The Economics of the
Transportation Firm

The Economics of the Transportation Firm

Market Structure and Industrial Performance

James T. Kneafsey
Massachusetts Institute
of Technology

Lexington Books
D.C. Heath and Company
Lexington, Massachusetts
Toronto   London

Library of Congress Cataloging in Publication Data

Kneafsey, James T.
    The economics of the transportation firm.

    Bibliography: p.
    1. Transportation—United States. I. Title.
HE203.K55   380.5'0973   73-12746
ISBN 0-669-90977-7

Copyright © 1974 by D.C. Heath and Company.

Published simultaneously in Canada.

Printed in the United States of America. 75-6522

International Standard Book Number: 0-669-90977-7

Library of Congress Catalog Card Number: 73-12746

To my parents

Contents

List of Figures

List of Tables

Preface

This book is a study of the firms comprising the transportation industries in the United States. Its focus is on the industrial organization aspects of the largest transportation firms. In particular, the book examines the market structures of the airline, railroad, and motor trucking industries and the ways in which the firms in these industries behave and perform.

Since very little attention has been given in the literatures of transportation, economics, or engineering to the topic of business firm behavior in transportation, the spark for this book came from my realization that very few individuals understood or appreciated the role of transportation firms in the overall system of transportation. Nowhere have I been able to find a document which centered on this topic.

The "theory of the firm" is at the heart of traditional microeconomics. In an appraisal of business firms' behavior, applied microeconomics attempts to model the attributes of the typical, unregulated firm. The usual way of treating regulated firms is to isolate their activities under the "economics of regulation." Unfortunately, the student of the regulated industries often becomes overwhelmed with the institutional issues of these industries and loses sight of the underlying theory in the process. A similar experience is shared by students of transportation, especially since the available menu of transportation texts in their nth editions usually emphasizes institutional and legal factors at the expense of theoretical and policy issues.

My view of transportation economics is that of an applied field which relies on the rigorous theory of microeconomics and the contemporary applications of econometric methods. From the point of view of the transportation firms, it is in many ways a subset of the "field" of industrial organization. Admittedly, many important problems and issues in transportation economics lie outside of industrial organization, for instance, local mass transit problems, user requirements, sources of tax revenues, and issues of equity. The unique approach taken in this book, however, is to isolate the managerial and organizational phenomena which can be observed in the behavior of transportation firms.

The book attempts to treat the industrial organization aspects of firms in the domestic transportation industries without overwhelming the reader with burdensome and nonessential citations and detail. Its major thrust is the demonstration of how microeconomic theory applies to transportation markets. From this thrust, its fundamental plea is to the independent regulatory commissions: that they simply investigate the microtheoretical properties of their cases in a more streamlined way as a basis for making better policy decisions. This task should not be difficult to accomplish because the foundations for analysis have been brought forth in the industrial organization field. At minimum, we should incorporate some of that field's findings, even though they may not be universally conclusive, into the economics of the transportation firms.

The microeconomic view of transportation firms taken in this book is comparatively new. The author's interest and belief in this approach originated in graduate school and increased with the encouragement of Richard A. Tybout, J. Hayden Boyd, Edgar M. Hoover, and Merrill J. Roberts.

The specific material for this book grew out of the contents of two courses which I developed originally on "The Economics of Control" and "Transportation Economics" at the University of Pittsburgh and then a subsequent graduate level course on "Market Structure and Economic Performance in the Transportation Industries" at MIT. I wish to express my thanks to Reuben Slesinger and Mark Perlman of the University of Pittsburgh and to A. Scheffer Lang, formerly of MIT, for allowing me the necessary latitude in developing the contents of these courses.

I also wish to thank H.W. Bruck, Paul O. Roberts and Joseph Sussman at MIT for providing research opportunities which allowed for certain ideas to be transformed into writing. Discussions with Wayne Pecknold, Michael Godfrey, Marvin Manheim, Robert Simpson, Nawal Taneja, and others sharpened my perspective of transportation systems analysis. I wish to acknowledge additional suggestions and comments on earlier portions of the manuscript from Paul W. MacAvoy, Morris Adelman, and James Sloss. Critical editorial assistance was gratefully received from Ephraim Gerber, Marty Blalock, and Penelope Rohrbach. I also am indebted to Nancy Neuman and Donna Martin for their generous assistance in typing the manuscript. Finally, I appreciate the guidance provided by my editor, Barbara Levey. Of course, full responsibility for any errors or shortcomings which may persist is mine.

The Economics of the
Transportation Firm

1 Introduction: The Domestic Transportation Industries

The industrial transportation facilities of the United States consist of various types of rights-of-way, terminal operations, vehicles which provide motive power and which contain space for passengers or commodities, communications equipment, and numerous forms of specialized occasional devices designed to improve the flow of transportation services or to respond to the needs of special types of passenger or freight traffic. The companies which provide these domestic transportation services are business enterprises, competing for the same financial and resource markets as other firms. Each company functions in a particular mode of transportation, where ideally each should carry that portion of the traffic it can best serve at the lowest total resource cost. For many years, however, practitioners have accepted the belief that some industries, in which competition is not fully effective, must be regulated by agencies of the federal government in order to protect the public interest. Those industries which have been subjected to public regulation are collectively referred to as the regulated industries. Domestic transportation comes under the heading of regulated industries and therein lies a set of dilemmas.

As commonly used, the phrase "regulated indusiries" refers to a diverse group of business operations which has been subjected to local, state, and federal regulation on matters of rates and services.[1] These industries typically are divided into two major classes: first, the public utilities—those enterprises supplying energy in the form of electricity and natural gas, communications services (telephone and telegraph) and water; and second, the transportation industries—those firms providing local, statewide and interregional transportation, such as airlines, railroads, motor freight carriers, bus companies, gas and oil pipelines, and water carriers.[a]

These industries differ in some generic ways from other industries in the economy. The principal historical difference is that the regulated industries, especially the public utilities, tend toward monopoly or, more accurately, that the firms in these industries allegedly operate more efficiently as monopolies.[b] The transportation industries also have been absorbed under this umbrella of monopolies, or in the case of the railroads, as "natural monopolies."[2] Yet the

[a]There are several other industries and activities which also are subject to varying degrees of regulation, notably: banking, corporate securities, radio and television broadcasting, and atomic energy at the federal level; and insurance and milk distribution at the state level.

[b]The issue of efficiency in the public utilities is a very complex topic and is beyond the scope of this book.

1

transportation industries have not displayed the same kinds of monopoly tendencies as public utilities, especially in the cases of motor trucking and domestic water tarnsportation. In fact, the extent to which the firms in the domestic transportation industries should be treated as part of the regulated industries (in the traditional sense) is the basic issue to which this book addresses itself. The book thus focuses on the industrial organization aspects of the firms comprising the domestic transportation industries.

No one can dispute that there is a strong degree of public interest attached to the services provided by the transportation industries. In practice, the public interest criterion is the primary legal basis for regulation in this country. The uniqueness of the transportation industries here contrasts with most other countries which have nationalized these industries. In the United States, there are two common characteristics which distinguish the transportation industries from all others: first, private ownership and management are predominant; and second, there exist varying degrees of public regulation in conjunction with the independent regulatory commissions.

This combination of private ownership and public control leads inevitably to conflict. The companies have been attempting to profitably offer services which are deemed essential to the economy and which are construed as quasi-public in nature.[3] As private and public interests clashed over the years, compromises quite often have been the ultimate outcomes—with both sectors suffering adverse consequences. Public regulation of the transportation industries became necessary, given that public policy required a restriction of competitive forces vis-à-vis a continuation of private ownership. The basic function of this book, then, is to explore the ways in which the transportation industries have been structured and how they have performed in economic terms within the framework of their regulatory environments.

The Role of Transportation Economics

Economics evolved in the late eighteenth and nineteenth centuries as a means to rationalize the historical development of market systems. The negotiating and controlling mechanisms in those centuries were the competitive markets and the systems of prices that emerged from the bargains between freely contracting buyers and sellers. Even today, the justification of the competitive market is still relevant to most advanced economies. For all the significant changes to which market economies have been subjected in practice during the twentieth century, the competitive market model has remained an important standard for the characteristics of an ideal economic system. Nonetheless, there are at least two sectors of the U.S. economy that the competitive market model cannot even purport to describe: the public sector, where the allocation of resources is determined mainly by political decisions, and the above regulated sector in which the organization and management are mostly private but the central economic decisions are subject to direct governmental regulation. In these sectors, the primary standard of reasonableness is not competition but rather direct governmental prescription of major characteristics of their market structure and economic performance.

The transportation industries are distinguished from other sectors of the economy by four principal components of this regulation: (1) control of entry, (2) fare and rate fixing, (3) the prescription of quality and conditions of service, and (4) the imposition of an obligation to serve all users under reasonable conditions. Transportation economics, then, is an analysis of the economics of that regulation—its structural and performance characteristics, its environmental conditions, and its statutory requirements.

In terms of economic analysis, one must distinguish between the different modes of transportation because the institutional arrangement, managerial practices, and market structure are very different in the air, rail, water, motor, and pipeline industries. The analysis must indicate the distinctions between passenger and freight traffic, between intercity and urban movements, and between domestic and international transportation. Even in the case of a single industry, the analyst must define the scope of his study very carefully. As an example, the analysis for evaluating TACV (Track Air Cushion Vehicle) would be very different from examining AMTRAK or previous intercity rail passenger service with conventional technology, because neither the immediate nor long-run effects of TACV are known.

It is essential for the analyst to specify every time the location, environment, and time period to which his analysis is applicable, especially since each economic analysis requires stringent assumptions about the constancy of all variables except the ones under focus.[c] Table 1-1 portrays the general scope of transportation economics, including the two basic ingredients of freight and passengers.

In terms of the scope of transportation economics, it also must be kept in mind that there are several components to the total transportation picture involving the actual users of transportation, the firms (carriers) which are providing the services, the extent of government agency participation, and the impacts on nonusers (often referred to as the public interest elements). An economic analysis conducted solely at the user level in urban transportation might suggest different policy implications than an analysis at the firm or agency level, since firms and users frequently have different interests and are striving for different objectives. For example, many riders in the Boston metropolitan area may be interested in free transit, but the MBTA (the local transit agency in Boston) cannot offer commuter services at zero fares unless large subsidies were involved. The cross-effects on nonusers as a result of the income transfers

---

[c]In technical terms, this feature is the "ceteris paribus" condition, whereby the analysis becomes one of partial equilibrium.

Table 1-1
The General Scope of Transportation Economics

Ingredients of Transportation Economics	Mode of Transportation
Passengers:	(1) Air
International	(2) Rail
Domestic	(3) Motor
Intercity	(a) Auto
Urban	(b) Bus
	(c) Truck
Commodities (Freight):	(d) Personal Rapid Transit
International	(4) Water
Domestic	(a) Inland
	(b) Ocean
	(5) Pipeline
	(6) New Technology
	(7) Dual Mode

necessary to pay for these subsidies and the increasing role of governmental involvement would complicate the analysis. In order to illustrate an overview of the scope of transportation economics, a flow chart of all the uses and sources of transportation (including international) in 1970 is shown in Figure 1-1.

The Domestic Transportation Industries

The American Trucking Associations estimated that motor carriers in 1971 moved 430 billion ton-miles of freight, accounting for 22.3 percent of the total of freight transport, as illustrated in Table 1-2. Of these 430 billion ton-miles, approximately 176 billion represented the intercity portion of freight transported by the Class I, II, and III motor carriers.[d] Note that the market share of motor carriers in comparison to that of the railroads has been rising steadily since 1945. The stabilization of the motor carriers' market share with respect to all modes around the 22 percent figure during the last decade is influenced by the increased movements of oil by the pipeline companies. The airlines' ton-mile market share has remained insignificant, although volume has quadrupled during the last decade.

The revenue distribution among the regulated freight carriers is more

[d]The larger remainder includes the intercity ton-miles of all private trucks and for-hire trucks not subject to economic regulation by the ICC and the intercity ton-miles of local ICC carriers.

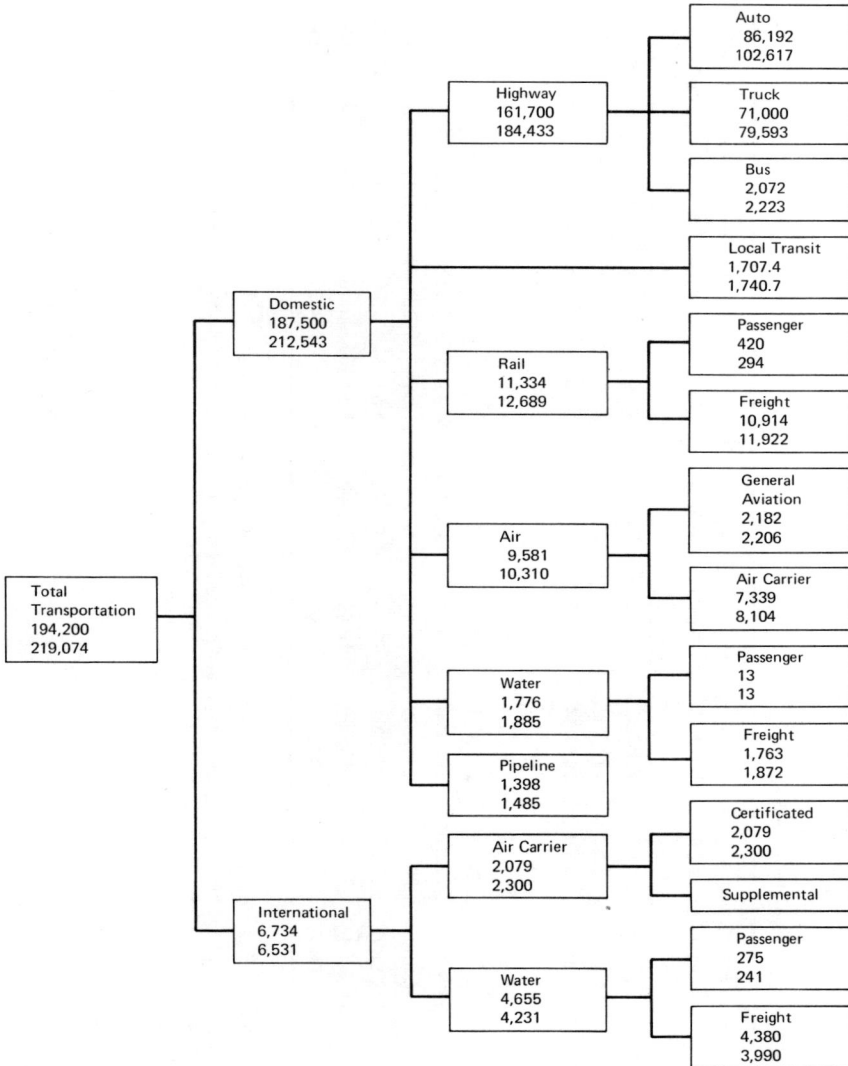

Figure 1-1. Modal Structure: Expenditures for Private Modes and Revenues of For-Hire Modes. Millions of Dollars, 1970—top figure in rectangle—and 1971—lower figure in rectangle. Sources: Institute for Defense Analysis, *Economic Characteristics of the Urban Public Transportation Industry* (Washington, D.C.: U.S. Government Printing Office, February 1972), p. 7; and *Summary of National Transportation Statistics*, Report No. DOT-TSC-OST-73-36 (Washington: U.S. Department of Transportation, November 1973), p. 8.

Table 1-2
Ton-Mile Distribution among Intercity Freight Carriers

Year	Railroads[a] Ton-Miles (Millions)	Railroads % of Total	Motor Carriers Ton-Miles (Millions)	Motor Carriers % of Total	Inland Waterways[b] Ton-Miles (Millions)	Inland Waterways % of Total	Pipelines (Oil) Ton-Miles (Millions)	Pipelines (Oil) % of Total	Airways[c] Ton-Miles (Millions)	Airways % of Total	Total[d] Ton-Miles (Millions)
1940	379,201	61.30	62,043	10.03	118,057	19.08	59,277	9.58	14	0.002	618,592
1945	690,809	67.26	66,948	6.52	142,737	13.90	126,530	12.32	91	0.009	1,027,115
1950	596,940	56.17	172,860	16.27	163,344	15.37	129,175	12.16	318	0.030	1,062,637
1955	631,385	49.53	223,254	17.51	216,508	16.98	203,244	15.94	481	0.038	1,274,872
1960	579,130	44.06	285,483	21.72	220,253	16.76	228,626	17.40	778	0.059	1,314,270
1965	708,700	43.25	359,218	21.92	262,421	16.01	306,393	18.70	1,910	0.120	1,638,642
1967	731,216	41.43	388,500	22.01	281,400	15.95	361,040	20.46	2,592	0.150	1,764,749
1968	756,800	41.16	396,300	21.55	291,409	15.85	391,300	21.28	2,805	0.160	1,838,614
1969	774,000	40.84	404,000	21.32	302,901	15.98	411,000	21.69	3,246	0.170	1,895,147
1970	768,000	39.74	412,000	21.32	318,000	16.46	431,000	22.30	3,408	0.180	1,932,408
1971[e]	742,500	38.45	430,000	22.26	307,000	15.90	448,000	23.20	3,700	0.190	1,931,200

aClass I and Class II Railroads.

bIncluding Great Lakes, but excluding deep sea ton-miles between mainland and Alaska, Hawaii and territories.

cScheduled domestic service, including mail and subsidy, express freight and excess baggage. Comparability of early data with 1950 and later years is limited due to the inclusion since that time of additional domestic air carrier services. Effective January 1, 1970, all travel between 48 states, Alaska, and Hawaii was reclassified as domestic service through the changes in 1969 and 1970.

dComponents may not add to total due to rounding.

eEstimates.

Sources: Interstate Commerce Commission, Bureau of Economics–*Transport Economics*, *ICC Annual Reports*; Federal Aviation Agency–*Statistical Handbook of Aviation*; Air Transport Association of America–*Facts and Figures about Air Transportation*; Civil Aeronautics Board–*Handbook of Airline Statistics*.

revealing. Table 1-3 shows that the operating revenues of motor carriers (Class I, II, and III) in 1971 were estimated at $16.7 billion, which represents a market share of 53.1 percent of all modes' revenues. Unlike the ton-mile distribution, the revenue market share of motor carriers has been increasing sharply during the last decade, both with respect to all modes and especially to that of the railroads. The railroads and the motor carriers clearly are the principal revenue generators in freight transport—together they are responsible for 92 cents of every freight transport revenue dollar.[e]

While the data in Tables 1-2 and 1-3 are not perfectly aligned, aggregate comparisons are interesting. The revenue distribution data show the benefits of relatively high-value commodities to the motor carrier industry: in 1971 these carriers generated 53.1 percent of all freight revenues stemming from carrying only 22.3 percent of the total volume. The impacts of high-value freight also are displayed by examining the airlines' shares for 1971: $766 million in revenues (or 2.4 percent of all freight revenues) were generated from just 3.7 billion ton-miles of air freight (or only 0.2 percent of all ton-miles). The converse side of the domestic freight market is the bulk, low-value area where the pipeline and inland waterway firms together account for 39.1 percent of all ton-miles but generate only a combined 5.6 percent of freight revenues.[f]

From the revenue side of the freight picture, the most important trend over the years has been the increasing dominance of the motor carrier industry.[4] This is especially important in view of the shifts in composition of the industry. Two trends stand out: first, a large increase in the number of Class I carriers; and second, a concomitant absolute decline in the number of the small carriers (see Table 1-4). The industry as a whole in 1971 encompassed more than 15,000 firms, of which 1,771 were Class I carriers and only 61 were publicly owned companies.[5]

In the airline industry, by far the largest portion of revenues stems from the intercity passenger market. Also, the airline industry has been capturing an increasing share of the intercity passenger market over the years (see Table 1-5).

In the railroad industry, the largest percentage of revenues comes from the freight sector. In fact, approximately 99 percent of all railroad revenues in 1972 were derived from this source.[g] For all practical purposes, private railroads really are not in the passenger business. The National Railroad Passenger Corporation (AMTRAK) has relieved the companies of their strictly legal burden of providing

---

[e]While the combined market share of railroads and motor carriers for freight revenues has remained invariant over the years (as illustrated in Table 1-3) around the 92 percent level, the same two modes combined share for ton-miles has declined gradually to its present level of about 61.7 percent (see Table 1-2).

[f]However, the revenue market share of the pipeline companies should very well increase during the next few years if regulatory constraints are relaxed.

[g]Four railroads did not join AMTRAK at its inception and still provide a limited passenger train service. These railroads are the Southern; Denver and Rio Grande Western; Chicago, Rock Island and Pacific; and Georgia Central.

Table 1-3
Revenue Distribution among Regulated Freight Carriers (Gross Operating Revenue[a] from Transportation of Goods)

	Railroads Class I & II		Motor Carriers Class I, II & III		Water Carriers Class A, B, C & Maritime[b]		Pipelines (Oil)		Airways[c]		Total[d]
	Thousands of Dollars	% of Total	Thousands of Dollar	% of Total	Thousands of Dollars	% of Total	Thousands of Dollars	% of Total	Thousands of Dollars	% of Total	Thousands of Dollars
1940	$ 3,686,375	75.43	$ 867,000	17.74	$ 85,394	1.75	$ 225,760	4.62	$ 22,719	0.46	$ 4,887,248
1945	6,748,528	78.65	1,406,300	16.39	74,314	0.87	304,268	3.55	48,827	0.55	8,580,237
1950	8,134,568	64.09	3,737,052	29.44	259,111	2.04	441,627	3.48	119,984	0.95	12,692,342
1955	8,888,122	57.04	5,535,209	35.53	321,403	2.06	677,605	4.35	158,711	1.02	15,581,050
1960	8,390,026	49.39	7,213,911	42.47	335,257	1.97	770,417	4.54	278,118	1.64	16,987,729
1965	9,286,628	44.15	10,068,243	47.86	314,070	1.49	903,817	4.30	463,327	2.20	21,036,085
1967	9,591,230	42.29	11,229,307	49.51	313,200	1.39	994,300	4.38	550,517	2.43	22,678,554
1968	10,247,197	41.22	12,655,351	50.91	319,500	1.29	1,023,000	4.11	615,127	2.47	24,860,175
1969	10,876,153	40.34	13,958,028	51.98	330,300	1.23	1,103,300	4.09	690,325	2.56	26,958,106
1970	11,100,000	39.93	14,400,000	51.80	400,000	1.44	1,188,254	4.27	709,598	2.55	27,797,852
1971[e]	12,200,000	38.82	16,700,000	53.14	479,000	1.52	1,284,000	4.09	766,366	2.44	31,429,366

aIncluded are revenues of federally regulated carriers only; a major portion of the traffic handled by motor and water carriers is not subject to this regulation—for example, not reflected are the revenues or value of service generated by intrastate, local and exempt for-hire and private motor carriers. The total value of all motor carrier services would approximately triple the $13.5 billion shown in 1969; consequently, this table does not compare the economic significance of different modes of transportation.

bIncludes only regulated water carriers, and excludes domestic traffic of regulated maritime carriers in coastal and intercoastal service for the years 1939-1947 (data not available for period). Because of changes of various kinds in regulation, reporting requirements, and statistical publication procedures, comparison of early data with 1951 and later years is not strictly valid.

cScheduled domestic service, including mail and subsidy, express freight and excess baggage. Comparability of early data with 1950 and later years is limited because of the inclusion since that time of additional domestic air carrier services. Effective January 1, 1970, all travel between 48 states, Alaska, and Hawaii was reclassified as domestic service through the changes in 1969 and 1970.

dComponents may not add to total due to rounding.

eEstimates.

Sources: Interstate Commerce Commission, Bureau of Economics—*Transport Economics, ICC Annual Reports*; Federal Aviation Agency—*Statistical Handbook of Aviation*; Air Transport Association of America—*Facts and Figures about Air Transportation*; Civil Aeronautics Board—*Handbook of Airline Statistics*.

Table 1-4
Number of Trucking Carriers by Size Class

Year	Class I $1,000,000 or More	Class II $200,000 to $1,000,000	Class III Under $200,000	Total
1957	933	2,055	14,779	17,767
1958	988	2,167	14,105	17,260
1959	1,009	2,256	14,383	17,648
1960	1,053	2,276	12,947	16,276
1961	1,106	2,336	12,556	15,998
1962	1,148	2,495	12,340	15,983
1963	1,175	2,533	11,910	15,618
1964	1,195	2,536	11,748	15,479
1965	1,250	2,615	11,700	15,565
1966	1,298	2,675	11,453	15,426
1967	1,389	2,769	11,238	15,396
	$1,000,000 or More	$300,000 to $1,000,000	Under $300,000	
1968	1,421	2,082	11,617	15,120
1969	1,503	1,998	11,706	15,207
1970	1,571	2,061	11,468	15,100
1971[a]	1,771	2,202	11,165	15,138

[a]Preliminary.
Source: Interstate Commerce Commission Statements No. 589 and 6406 and American Trucking Associations *American Trucking Trends* 1972 ed., p. 10.

Table 1-5
Airline Market Share of Domestic Intercity Passenger Miles for Selected Years[a]

Year	Air Market Share (%)
1939	2.3
1949	11.4
1955	32.9
1958	43.3
1960	43.9
1965	58.3
1968	72.5
1971	76.4

[a]For revenue passenger miles; excludes the auto mode.
Source: ICC Bureau of Economics and Statistics, various reports, 1972.

intercity passenger service, but there still remain the problems of reimbursements and operations conflicts (especially with the Penn Central). The commuter business is a totally separate problem: there is no conceivable reason why a railroad would naturally choose to offer this type of service, except for the burden of past regulatory imposition.[h] A listing of the regulatory jurisdiction for the various modes and for other selected industries appears in Table 1-6.

Any contemporary study of transportation requires an analysis of the issues which have become more complex and more diverse than ever. The various interactions among passengers, shippers, carriers, and government agencies have produced confusion, dismay, generally poor financial returns, and extreme concern for the future. A detailed description of the structural conditions in the three prominent transportation industries (including airlines-intercity passenger, railroads-intercity freight, and motor trucking-primarily intercity freight) appears in the following chapter.

Summary of the Contents

Since this book focuses on the industrial organization aspects of U.S. firms in the domestic transportation industries, various structural characteristics (such as size of firm, distribution of firms by size, market conditions, entry barriers, mergers, etc.), and selected performance measures of the carriers (such as rate of return criteria, operational measures, research and development impacts, etc.) will be analyzed in Chapters 2 and 3. The effects of regulation on market structure, performance, and various public policy issues will be examined in Chapter 4. Since industrial organization is concerned with matters of economic policy, which ultimately attempts to provide insights into questions such as the optimal forms of market structure on economic growth, the impacts of less regulation on resource allocation, and the effects of large-size companies on economic efficiency, Chapter 5 will investigate the existence of policy in national transportation issues and the need for practical transportation goals.

While an analysis of firms in the transportation industries has an empirical focus, research on these questions also requires a strong underlying theoretical structure if results applicable for policy are to be evaluated meaningfully. Chapter 6 therefore relates traditional microeconomic theory to the firms in the transportation industries and portrays the behavior of individuals in the transportation firms in terms of the particular phenomena of alienation, motivation, participation, and organization. Chapter 7 concludes the book by forecasting changes for the transportation industries in the long run and by exploring the requirements for more effective performance. In essence, the material in the book then includes: market structure and performance; theories

---

[h]It must be remembered that individual railroad firms initially chose to offer commuter-type service and at one time did experience a profitable return.

Table 1-6
Selected Data for Federal Independent Regulatory Commissions

Agency	Year Estab.	Number of Members	Term. Year	Staff Size	1967 Fiscal Budget (Millions of Dollars)	Jurisdiction
Interstate Commerce Commission	1887	11	7	1,929	$27.2	Railroads; motor carriers; inland waterways; oil pipelines; express companies; freight forwarders
Civil Aeronautics Board	1938	5	6	770	11.3	Airlines
Securities and Exchange Commission	1934	5	5	1,360	16.7	Securities and financial markets; electric and gas utility holding companies
Federal Power Commission	1920, 1930	5	5	1,131	14.2	Electric power; natural gas and natural gas pipelines; water-power sites
Federal Communications Commission	1934	7	7	1,458	17.9	Radio; television; telephone; telegraph; cables

Source: The Budget of the United States Government, Fiscal Year 1969, Appendix (Washington, D.C.: U.S. Government Printing Office, 1968).

of market behavior; the economics of regulation in transportation; and theories of behavior as applied to individuals and firms in the transportation industries.

Notes

1. One of the best sources on this topic is Charles F. Phillips, Jr., *The Economics of Regulation: Theory and Practice in the Transportation and Public Utility Industries*, rev. ed. (Homewood, Ill.: Richard D. Irwin, Inc., 1969).

2. Again, see Phillips, *Economics of Regulation*, pp. 4 ff. and p. 21.

3. In the famous *Smyth v. Ames* case, Justice Harlan argued that "a railroad is a public highway . . . and performs a function of the State." 169 U.S. 466, 544 (1898).

4. For a thorough classification of the detailed laws and regulations governing specific vehicles, length, weight and speed limitations, see *Trucking Business* 67 (October 1973).

5. These sixty-one carriers include those whose stocks are publicly owned or are subsidiaries of corporations whose stocks are listed on a national security exchange or traded over-the-counter. The average operating revenues for these sixty-one carriers in 1971 amounted to $73.3 million. Sources: *Transport Statistics, Moody's Transportation Manual* and *Trincs Red Book—Trucking Industry*.

2

Market Structure in the Transportation Industries

An ideal transportation system should be strong, efficient, and financially stable. In order to approach these global objectives, regulatory policies must be neutral among the competing carriers. No regulatory commission should provide an unfair advantage to a carrier or to an industry through special promotion, user charges, subsidy, taxation, or economic regulation. But in practice, the development of a neutral government policy is easier discussed than achieved.

Regulation of the transportation industries has developed on the belief that the competitive model cannot be relied on to serve the public interest.[1] In some markets, too little competition may exist, leading to exploitation of shippers; in other markets, too much competition may prevail, inducing low profits, market instability, and wasted resources. Examples of both situations have appeared in the past history of the transportation industries under varying degrees of regulation.

The crucial question of public policy in transportation pertains to the conditions which exist in the transportation industries today: To what extent is competition workable, especially if, as most economists suggest, government regulation were relaxed? To provide a basis for analyzing this question, an examination of the market structures of the various modes of transportation is the first step.

The typical book references to the structure and performance of firms in imperfectly competitive industries are rather sterile because they only suggest in a general manner that a range of possible types of behavior in imperfect markets may exist, and they do not indicate the methods and data sources on which these conclusions actually are derived. The basic analytical models—competition and monopoly—are not directly applicable in the analysis or appraisal of the behavior and performance of firms in an imperfectly competitive industry such as transportation. These models do, nevertheless, provide points of departure which can assist in answering many questions that are important for an appraisal of the operations and public policy implications of each industry:

1. Is the present size distribution of firms in the industry consistent with that necessary to achieve maximum efficiency?
2. Is there an "optimal-sized" firm?
3. What are the dynamics of optimal size in the long run?
4. What are the efficient means of attaining optimal size?

15

Do industries dominated by a few sellers earn more than normal profits and thereby distort the economic allocation of scarce resources? Are larger firms necessary in order to realize the advantages of economies of scale? As firms grow larger, do they dominate markets by virtue of their increasing size or by continued progressiveness and efficiency?

As long as existing technology is used in the most productive way, markets should perform more efficiently the greater the competition; or in the words of Morris Adelman: "Competition works only because everyone is trying to escape it, and to find some trade or other source of above-normal return."[2] In fact, the historical attempts to protect competitors probably has inhibited competition and thereby prevented the best use of existing technology or even the optimal rate of innovation.[3] The measurement of the success of competition (whether it be in terms of the number of participants, larger size firms, or a different size distribution in a given market) on technical change or the rate of innovation depends on the nature of the industry itself, the location of the market, the time period, the innovation process and the characteristics of the service (or product) offered.

The elements of the transportation industries can cover a broad front. In its widest sense, the transportation industries would include those firms producing equipment and services of the following types:

Rail: Freight; passenger; track and structures; rolling stock; terminal facilities; containerization; TOFC (Trailer-on-Flatcar).

Motor: Highway trucks and semitrailers; passenger automobiles; buses; taxicabs.

Air: Freight; passenger; helicopters; aircraft; tourist services.

Water: Bulk-cargo ships; river tows; towboats; barges.

Pipeline: Commodities; pumping-station equipment; rights-of-way.

Other: Hydrofoils; ferries; conveyors; aerial tramways (cableways); TACV; dual-mode systems; personal rapid transit systems.

Firms which participate in any markets offering the above transportation activities can be considered a part of the transportation industries. Yet the listing represents a polymorphous group because many of the companies are suppliers or users or accessorial carriers to the primary firms. The infrastructure of domestic transportation depends on the primary firms: those companies who by their legal status and statutory rights are common carriers, which means that they are in the business of providing a transportation service at reasonable rates (or fares) to all who request the service.

The focus in this book is on the economics of the transportation firm: namely, the common carrier of domestic transportation service. Practically all railroads in the United States are common carriers. In the motor carrier industry, there are three types of carriers: first, the common carrier; second, the contract carriers, which are also in business for compensation but serve a restricted clientele; and third, the proprietary or private carrier, which provides its own transportation and does not hire itself out to carry anyone else's traffic for compensation. In the airline industry, the predominant traffic is of a common carriage type, whereas in the water carrier field, one finds mostly contract or private carriage. While pipeline companies by statute are common carriers, in practice they are either contract or private carriers because they only serve a very limited number of customers.

Every freight transportation transaction or contract involves three sets of participants: (1) the direct participants—the carriers, shippers, and consigners; (2) ancillary parties—banks, financial and insurance companies, customs agencies, and so forth, each of whom deals with document exchanges rather than cargo activity; and (3) indirect parties—forwarders, port authorities, environmental groups, competitive shippers, and so forth. While each of these participants represents an important cog in the movement of commodities, the focus in this book is on the common carrier alone, whether the carrier is incorporated to conduct business in the freight sector, passenger sector, or both. In particular, the analysis is limited to the three largest revenue industries in domestic transportation: airlines, railroads, and motor trucking. While pipelines and inland waterways are important transportation industries, they are relatively remote from the mainstream of the public eye and have been discussed adequately elsewhere. Furthermore, it is anticipated that the inferences from the analyses of market structure and industrial performance in the three large revenue industries are relatively more important to examine in light of contemporary public policy issues.

Fundamental Terminology

In every specialized area of knowledge, there are terms which possess particular and occasionally very specific meanings. Seven terms are used repeatedly throughout this book, namely: *industry, firm, market, structure, behavior, performance*, and *transportation*. Consequently, a brief glossary of the meanings attached to these terms might be helpful to the reader.

Industry. An industry usually is composed of a group of firms (or establishments) primarily in the same or closely related types of business activity. An ideal classification of an industry should include all firms engaged in the provision of the same type of service or the production of similar products. Since each of the transportation industries is regulated by an independent commission, the definitions of airlines, railroads, and motor carriers are straightforward and will be discussed below.[4]

Firm. The firm is viewed as a collection of particular resources which can be used either for producing output (that is, providing transportation services) or for training new resources. The firm, then, is the traditional organization, incorporated with a state charter and in business for profit. Since the emphasis is on the industrial organization aspects of transportation, the firm is the carrier of rail, trucking, or air transport services, respectively, as defined by the entry conditions specified by the relevant regulatory agency.

Market. Quite often, one refers to the market economy without paying particular attention to the meaning of the word. In this book, a market includes all the participants (buyers and sellers), actual and potential, of a particular transportation service or set of services. There are several levels of markets in domestic transportation: fixed (or contractual), local, city-pair, regional, and national. Due to the geographical constraints imposed by the regulatory agencies, an individual firm's competition with other firms in its industry and with firms in other modes may be limited to specific markets. Other regulatory constraints either may impede any form of competition or may prolong excess competition in certain markets.

Structure. A large effort by economists interested in industrial organization has been devoted to the measurement of structural characteristics of markets or industries. Here, structure refers to those factors that will determine and effect the performance of firms in the transportation industries. Market structure is an aggregate concept, referring to certain ways in which each transportation industry is structured or aligned. In his well-known book on industrial organization, Joe Bain claims that the salient dimensions of market structure pertain to concentration, product differentiation, and entry conditions. In explaining his choice of a small number of elements, Bain states:

At times, market structure has been defined much more broadly.... So construed, market structure could embrace every objective circumstance—psychological, technological, geographical or institutional—that might conceivably influence market behavior.... We do not espouse this concept of market structure here because a very loose and frequently ambiguous use of the idea of structure is involved, and also because meaningful intermarket comparisons and meaningful generalizations about the influence of structure on behavior are effectively forestalled if the content of "structure" is made so comprehensive that no two markets can be viewed as structurally alike.[5]

Other researchers prefer to use a larger list of elements to denote market structure and present evidence to substantiate their views.[6] A further discussion of this topic appears below.

Behavior: In actual markets, expectations, uncertainties, market control, and the rate structure are very significant influences on firms' activities. Market behavior (loosely analogous to market conduct) refers to the manner in which firms "behave" within the context of their market structure; or as Bain, in his earlier monograph, describes it: "patterns ... which enterprises follow in adapting or adjusting to the markets in which they sell (or buy)."[7]

Performance. A primary societal concern should relate to how an industry performs in terms of its efficiency, progressiveness, stability, and true worth. The concept of economic performance, then, refers to the economic results that flow from an industry. Bain lists five measures:

1. The height of price relative to the average cost of production
2. The relative efficiency of production so far as this is influenced by the scale or size of plants and firms (relative to the most efficient) and by the extent of excess capacity
3. The size of sales promotion costs relative to the costs of production
4. The character of the product, including choice of design, level of quality, and variety of product within any market
5. The rate of progressiveness of the firm and industry in developing both products and techniques of production, relative to evidently attainable rates and relative to the costs of progress.[8]

In general, performance criteria reflect economic yardsticks. A detailed discussion of these and other measures of industrial performance appears in Chapter 3.

Transportation. As stated previously, the emphasis in this book is on the firms which offer transportation services (freight and passenger) in the domestic markets.[9] The primary slant is from the side of industrial organization. In particular, the analyses examine market structure and industrial performance in the airline, railroad, and motor trucking industries.

Market Structure

In a strictly economic sense, the transportation industries should behave similarly to other industries, and the firms which compose the transportation industries should perform similarly to other firms in the nonregulated industries. All are competing for the same investment sources in the various money (short-term) and capital (long-term) markets. From the production side, different industries and their firms have different technological characteristics and therefore may require different production functions to portray their behavior accurately.[a] But each firm's activities a priori are capable of specification by an existing production function form, subject to subsequent empirical verification:

The basic questions about market structure concern what it is, what determines it, and what effects it has. Conceptual and econometric answers to the questions are still formative . . . and structure-performance relations in large areas of market activity remain conjectural.[10]

In transportation, it is relatively easier to develop a set of industry definitions. The industry boundaries are usually determined by regulatory statute. In the following sectors are brief summaries and commentaries on the market structures of the railroad, motor trucking, and airline industries.

The Railroad Industry

Under the accounting system prescribed by the Interstate Commerce Commission, railroad operating revenues and expenses are separated between freight and passenger services so that a net railway operating income for each service can be calculated. There is a direct assignment of expenses regarded as solely related to one service or the other; common or joint expenses are apportioned according to statistical formulae devised by the ICC. The common cost allocations have been the subject of much controversy and appear to warrant a change.[11]

Railroads are classified by the Interstate Commerce Commission into two size classes: Class I railroads, those with annual operating revenues exceeding $5 million; and Class II railroads, the remainder. Table 2-1 shows some selected statistics for the Class I railroads over a four-year period, 1968-1972; the table also allows comparisons among the three major districts into which the ICC divides the Class I roads. By far, the Class I roads are the more important: in 1972 there were 65 Class I and 205 Class II railroads, but the Class I companies accounted for 99 percent of the industry's line-haul traffic and 97 percent of total operating revenues. Even within the Class I scheme, concentration is high; the large railroads, as depicted in Table 2-2, controlled nearly 80 percent of the mileage operated and collected over 60 percent of the freight revenues. If one includes total operating revenues, the absolute size of the largest railroads is substantial, as Table 2-3 indicates.

From a competitive point of view, most efforts are intramodal and related to

[a]Recent evidence in the growing interest of the appropriate theoretical and empirical specifications of particular production functions suggests that the answer depends on the industry under observation. Alternative parametric forms have been derived, analyzed, and tested on various bodies of data (both time series and cross-sectional). The general conclusions to be drawn from these statistical tests is that certain industries specified by the Cobb-Douglas (CD) form exhibit greater explanatory powers, others by the Constant-Elasticity-of-Substitution (CES) form. See C.A.K. Lowell, "CES and VES Production Functions in a Cross-Section Context," *Journal of Political Economy* 81 (May/June 1973), pp. 705-720.

Table 2-1
Selected Railroad Statistics: 1969-1972

Year	District	Operating Revenues[a]	Operating Expenses[a]	Net Railway Operating Income[a,b]	Rate of Return[c]	Revenue Ton-Miles[d]	Freight Car Miles[d]
1969	U.S.	$11.4	$ 9.1	0.65	2.36	768	30.3
	Eastern	4.3	3.5	0.12	1.10	260	9.7
	Southern	1.9	1.4	0.18	4.17	139	5.1
	Western	5.2	4.1	0.35	2.81	369	15.5
1970	U.S.	11.9	9.6	0.49	1.73	764	29.9
	Eastern	4.5	3.8	(0.10)	def.	254	9.5
	Southern	2.0	1.5	0.21	4.50	140	5.1
	Western	5.4	4.3	0.38	3.02	370	15.2
1971	U.S.	12.7	10.1	0.70	2.49	739	29.2
	Eastern	4.6	3.9	(0.03)	def.	225	8.7
	Southern	2.2	1.6	0.24	4.83	140	5.3
	Western	5.9	4.6	0.49	3.92	374	15.2
1972	U.S.	13.4	10.6	0.84	2.95	778	30.3
	Eastern	4.8	3.9	0.05	0.44	231	8.8
	Southern	2.3	1.7	25.00	5.17	149	5.6
	Western	6.3	4.9	53.00	4.19	398	15.9

[a]In billions of dollars.

[b]Net railway operating income is the remainder of operating revenues after deducting operating expenses, taxes, and rents for equipment and joint facilities, but before recording nonoperating income and deducting fixed charges, such as interest or debt and rents for leased lines.

[c]In percent: the relationship of net railway operating income to net investment in transportation property.

[d]In billions.

Source: Association of American Railroads, *Yearbook of Railroad Facts* (1973 edition).

city-pair markets, where usually the number of participants is few.[12] This fact suggests that the market structure of the railroad industry is one of oligopoly, with intramodal competition occurring only over the major city-pair markets.

From a financial point of view, at least twenty-five of the Class I railroads are in difficulty. The situation is especially serious in the Northeast. One can quickly notice from Table 2-1 that the rates of return are less than competitive with other industries.

It is not surprising that several railroads in the Northeast are bankrupt.[b]

[b]The bankrupt Class I railroads in the Northeast at the end of 1973 were the following: Penn Central (including New Haven), Lehigh Valley, Reading, Central of New Jersey, Erie Lackawanna, and Boston & Maine.

Table 2-2
Operating Freight Revenues: Class I Railroads for 1972[a]

Large Size Railroads

Atchison, Topeka &		Illinois Central Gulf	446.3
Santa Fe	794.0	Louisville & Nashville	447.5
Baltimore & Ohio	484.8	Missouri Pacific	434.6
Burlington Northern	956.2	Norfolk & Western	765.3
Chicago & Northwestern	322.7	Penn Central	1,606.5
Chicago, Milwaukee,		Seaboard Coast Line	546.6
St. Paul & Pacific	292.2	Southern	455.9
Chicago, Rock Island		Southern Pacific	1,092.3
& Pacific	288.2	Union Pacific	743.8
Erie Lackawanna	233.0		

Medium Size Railroads[b]

Boston & Maine	64.3	Missouri-Kansas-Texas	76.3
Central of Georgia	79.1	Reading	90.2
Cincinnati, New Orleans		St. Louis-San	
& T.P.	73.7	Francisco	221.3
Denver & Rio Grande		St. Louis Southwestern	150.5
Western	109.9	Soo Line	137.5
Grand Trunk Western	86.6	Texas & Pacific	104.7
Kansas City Southern	101.4	Western Pacific	85.5

Small Size Railroads[b,c]

Alabama Great Southern	48.2	Elgin, Joliet & Eastern	48.3
Bangor & Aroostook	13.1	Florida East Coast	38.4
Bessemer & Lake Erie	43.9	Fort Worth & Denver	
Central of New Jersey	29.8[d]	Lehigh Valley	49.2
Central of Vermont	9.6	Long Island	8.6[d]
Chicago & Eastern		Main Central	27.7
Illinois	39.0[d]	Monon	8.3[d]
Clinchfield	39.8	Norfolk Southern	15.0[e]
Colorado & Southern	26.5	Northwestern Pacific	14.0
Delaware & Hudson	40.9	Pittsburgh & Lake Erie	35.5
Detroit, Toledo & Ironton	40.6	Richmond, Fredericks-	
Duluth, Missabe & Iron		burg & Potomac	23.7
Range	42.3	Western Maryland	45.8

[a]In millions of dollars.
[b]Some Class I railroads reported here are operated as subsidiaries of larger companies.
[c]The table excludes 12 other very small Class I railroads.
[d]Represents a decline in revenues from 1968.
[e]Acquired by Southern Railway, November 1973.
Sources: Interstate Commerce Commission, Forms OS-A, OS-B and OS-C; American Association of Railroads, *Operating and Traffic Statistics* (1972), June 1973.

Among the more frequently stated explanations for this dilemma is the federal government support from general funds in the federal budget for airports, waterways, the merchant marine, and their support systems—competitors in the broad sense to the railroads. Also, the bitter polemics of featherbedding have

Table 2-3
Operating Revenues of the Largest Railroad Firms for 1972

Firm	Operating Revenues
Penn Central Transportation	$1,825.5
Southern Pacific	1,449.4
Burlington Northern	1,195.0
Seaboard Coast Line Industries	1,122.1
Union Pacific	1,094.4
Chesapeake & Ohio Railway	1,025.4
Santa Fe Industries	972.8
Norfolk & Western Railway	850.8
Southern Railway	723.8
Missouri Pacific System	642.9

Source: *Fortune*, July 1973, pp. 130-131. Reprinted by permission from the 1973 Fortune Directory; © 1973 Time Inc.

perpetuated and deepened traditional rifts between management and labor. Management itself either has been mediocre in quality or simply unable to cope with the irretrievable chain of circumstances that have beset the industry. Some claim that property taxes have been inordinately high, resulting in an erosion of each company's solvency. And then there is the ubiquitous imputation of blame to the ICC for forcing the railroads to maintain uneconomic services far beyond their justified retention.[13]

It may be more surprising that there are profitable railroads in the region, for example, the Chesapeake and Ohio Railway, the Baltimore & Ohio Railroad, and the Norfolk and Western Railway. Even in the bankrupt companies the survival of the operations is a tribute to the portion of the industry which is inherently efficient and to that segment of labor and management to which railroading is a way of life rather than merely a job. Even so, the survival of the bankrupt firms without external assistance is not assured unless the impending legislation is effective over the long run.

Various proposals have been put forth to resolve the current dilemma in the structure of railroad companies in the northeastern United States. While each of these proposals may have contained specific advantages for certain segments of the industry, it is possible that none of them actually will provide any practical remedies for returning the northeastern companies to viability in the long run. The central theme of all the proposed legislation is to "rationalize" the northeastern railroads by discontinuing service on, or by abandoning, approximately 15,000 miles of low-density trackage.

From a synthesis of these proposals, one study suggests a more comprehensive solution containing the additional advantage of reliance on market forces.[14] The outstanding feature of a market-oriented approach is that continuous adjustments to future economic changes can always be insured and promoted by the mechanisms of supply and demand. With this approach, it should not be necessary for Congress or the regulatory agencies to be periodically called upon to revamp the rail network whenever new crises arise. The recent national surge to conserve and to preserve energy dictates that careful social and economic considerations be afforded to the implementation of the restructured railroads, whatever shape they may take.

The drift of the current congressional restructuring program appears to lean toward the establishment of a large, single rail system (to be called the Consolidated Railroad Corporation) which would survive the financially troubled yet still competitive northeastern railroads. The direct and peripheral impacts of the new system on the profitable railroads (both large and small) contiguous to the Northeast are unknown. Without additional empirical evidence, there still may be a niche in the national rail network for small, closely managed and competitive companies.

The Motor Trucking Industry

The motor trucking industry encompasses a very large number of firms (see the discussion in the previous chapter in Table 1-3). Many of these firms, however, are relatively huge, as suggested by an array of the ten largest trucking firms, ranked by operating revenues (see Table 2-4). The yardstick of performance in the industry is the operating ratio (see Table 2-5), from which a rate of return

Table 2-4
Operating Revenues of the Largest Trucking Firms for 1972[a]

Firm	Operating Revenues
Consolidated Freightways	$591.1
Roadway Express	373.5
Leaseway Transportation	363.1
National City Lines	285.5
Yellow Freight System	258.6
McLean Trucking	195.1
Allied Van Lines	187.3
Associated Transport	143.7
Transcon Lines	128.7
Bekins	126.9

[a]In thousands of dollars; includes those revenues from nontransportation activities and sales from discontinued operations when they are published; all companies derived at least 85 percent of their operating revenues from carrier operations.
Source: *Fortune*, July 1973, pp. 130-131. Reprinted by permission from the 1973 Fortune Directory; ©1973 Time Inc.

Table 2-5

Operating Ratios for the Class I and II Intercity Motor Common Carriers[a]

Year	Operating Ratio
1945	99.2
1950	93.2
1955	95.8
1960	97.5
1965	94.7
1967	96.2
1968	95.0
1969	95.7
1970	96.2
1971	94.1

[a]The operating ratio is the percentage relationship of total operating expenses to gross revenues. For example, the operating ratio of 94.1 in 1971 indicates that the expenses of the carriers absorbed 94.1 percent of their revenues, leaving 5.9 percent net revenue from each dollar of gross revenues, prior to making nonoperating adjustments such as deductions for net interest and income taxes.

Source: Official Reports of the Motor Common Carriers to the Interstate Commerce Commission and American Trucking Associations, *American Trucking Trends* (1972 ed.).

can be calculated. The industry in the broadest sense includes almost 20 million trucks (see Table 2-6). In addition to the intercity carriers, there are thousands of motor carriers engaged in intrastate commerce, in hauling exempt agricultural commodities, and in private carriage.

During recent months various pieces of legislation have been introduced to the Congress with the intention of "opening up" numerous city-pair markets to a larger number of competitors. Needless to say, the large-sized trucking companies do not favor the tenor of this legislation and have been lobbying strongly against it.[15] The lobbying effort has been conducted by the firms themselves and through the American Trucking Associations (the industry lobby group), which presumably shares all trucking interests but in practice represents the interests of the larger companies. The ludicrousness of certain portions of the rate structure in the motor carrier industry is a well known and well documented topic. The likelihood of changes in the rate structure by the ICC or by the Congress at this time is only a matter of conjecture.

The Airline Industry

The airline industry is characterized by large private investments in equipment and facilities, despite the fact that airports and many supporting airway features are publicly financed. The modern fleet of aircraft represents expensive outlays

Table 2-6
Distribution of Trucks by Type of Vehicle and Use, 1972[a]

Trucks and Combinations	Private[b]		For-Hire		Total	
	Number	% of Total	Number	% of Total	Number	% of Total
Single Unit Trucks— 2 axles	17,486,200	93.8	331,200	38.6	17,817,400	91.4
3 axles	633,800	3.4	53,300	6.2	687,100	3.5
All Single Unit Trucks	18,120,000	97.2	384,500	44.8	18,504,500	94.9
Combinations— 3 axles	111,900	0.6	78,100	9.1	190,000	1.0
4 axles	205,000	1.1	161,500	18.8	366,500	1.9
5 or more axles	205,100	1.1	233,900	27.3	439,000	2.2
All Combinations	522,000	2.8	473,500	55.2	995,500	5.1
Total	18,642,000	100.0	858,000	100.0	19,500,000	100.0

[a]The distribution being used in this table is based on the *1967 Census of Transportation*, "Truck Inventory and Use Survey," Table 20.

[b]Of the 18,642,000 private trucks, about 3,500,000 are farm trucks.

Source: American Trucking Associations, *American Trucking Trends* (1972 ed.).

for equipment and requires an elaborate array of instrumentation and technical personnel to maintain its operation at maximum levels of safety and convenience.

The major classes of domestic air carriers are the trunklines, local service carriers, air commuters, and supplementary (or "nonskeds") carriers.[c] The trunks dominate the industry, with the Big Four (American, Eastern, TWA, and United) accounting for roughly two-thirds of all revenue passenger-miles.[d] Table 2-8 displays the rates of return for the trunklines and the local service carriers for 1965-1970. Notice that the rates have been declining significantly and have remained low during 1971 and 1972 (although the official data are not yet available at the time of this writing).

The best source for the names and initial routes of the United States domestic airlines is Almarin Phillips's monograph[16] which lists all the carriers analogous to the domestic trunklines which entered scheduled operations prior to 1938. An excellent source on the development of the local service carriers is a recent book by Eads.[17] The local service carriers (originally called "feeders" and sometimes "regionals") were created by the CAB after World War II for the specific purpose of furnishing local feeder air service. While nineteen carriers

[c]This classification excludes helicopter carriers, seaplane service, and all-cargo lines.

[d]The trunk carriers are those certificated in 1938 under the "grandfather" provisions of the Civil Aeronautics Act, Section 401 (e)(1). Table 2-7 shows the changes in the trunklines from that time to the present.

Table 2-7
Domestic Trunk Airlines, 1938-1973

Carrier	Year of Trunk Line Operations[a]
American Airlines	1938-
Eastern Air Lines	1938-
Trans-World Airlines	1938-
United Air Lines	1938-
Braniff Airways	1938-
Continental Air Lines	1938-
Delta Air Lines	1938-
National Airlines	1938-
Northwest Airlines	1938-
Western Air Lines	1938-
Capital Airlines[b]	1938-1960
Chicago and Southern Air Lines[c]	1938-1952
Colonial Airlines[d]	1939-1955
Inland Air Lines[e]	1938-1951
Mid-Continent Airlines[f]	1938-1951
Northeast Airlines[g]	1938-1972

[a]From 1938 to last full year of operation; names given are of most recent vintage.
[b]Absorbed by United Air Lines, June 1961.
[c]Absorbed by Delta Air Lines, May 1953.
[d]Absorbed by Eastern Air Lines, June 1956.
[e]Absorbed by Western Air Lines, April 1952.
[f]Absorbed by Braniff Airways, August 1952.
[g]Operated as Boston–Maine Airways, 1936 to 1938; absorbed by Delta Air Lines, August 1972.
Source: *Air Carrier Financial Statistics* (various years).

were originally certificated as local service carriers,[18] only eight remain, following the absorption of Mohawk Airlines by Allegheny Airlines in 1972 (see Table 2-8). A narrow definition of the domestic airline industry, then, would include the trunk carriers and the local service carriers. Clearly this segment of the industry is dominant in terms of any market structure proxy for size, whether it be operating revenues, passenger-miles, or assets.

A third sector of the airline industry pertains to the synonymous terms: commuter air carriers, third-level carrier, or air taxi. The commuter air-carrier industry has played an increasingly significant role in the provision of air transportation to small cities. Part 298 of the Civil Aeronautics Board's *Economic Regulations* designates air taxi operators as a class of air carriers which, among other things, "do not directly or indirectly utilize in air

Table 2-8

Rate of Return on Adjusted Investment, Certificated Route Air Carriers, Calendar Years 1965-1970

Carrier	1965	1966	1967	1968	1969	1970
			Year (Including Investment Tax Credit)			
Total Certificated Route Air Carriers	14.07	13.03	9.85	6.15	4.16	1.02
Domestic Operations of the Big Four						
American	10.51	19.09	7.93	5.98	6.64	−1.23
Eastern	11.54	6.01	6.46	0.77	2.99	3.65
TWA	11.01	7.65	4.45	1.72	1.45	−8.32
United	9.96	7.46	9.18	5.03	5.99	−1.13
Domestic Operations of the Other Trunks						
Braniff	16.15	16.03	2.20	5.28	6.22	1.79
Continental	19.82	21.84	14.47	5.72	4.73	5.43
Delta	24.63	29.86	19.97	15.97	14.16	13.26
National	20.01	16.31	17.94	13.61	9.96	−0.53
Northeast	−	3.73	−15.47	1.11	−66.85	−57.08
Northwest	21.05	16.60	15.00	11.23	8.96	−7.95
Western	15.43	16.69	11.51	7.25	−0.24	3.96
Local Service Carriers[a]						
Allegheny	10.18	7.38	4.36	2.97	2.85	6.74
Frontier	12.70	11.83	4.60	−3.34	−11.53	−0.70
Mohawk	15.97	4.39	3.61	−2.24	0.18	−9.39
North Central	12.02	10.36	8.49	5.15	2.95	8.26
Ozark	11.17	10.99	8.20	4.55	−0.03	2.59
Piedmont	15.01	8.01	10.68	5.11	4.15	3.21
Southern	15.27	10.95	2.43	3.50	3.20	7.21
Texas International	14.00	9.41	4.56	1.89	−5.75	−13.22
Pan American	13.41	15.56	10.53	7.56	−0.17	−0.57

[a]Excludes Air West.

Source: Civil Aeronautics Board, *Handbook of Airline Statistics*, 1971 ed.

transportation large aircraft (other than turbojet aircraft authorized for use under certain conditions), and do not hold a certificate of public convenience and necessity or other economic authority issued by the Board." Commuter air carrier is defined as "an air taxi operator which either performs at least five round trips per week between two or more points and publishes flight schedules which specify the times, days of the week and places between which such flights are performed, or transports mail by air pursuant to a current contract with the Post Office Department." Air-taxi operators are therefore exempted from economic regulation.

Since Part 298 became effective in 1952, several changes have occurred. Originally, air taxi operators were not permitted to carry mail or to provide frequent service on markets which were served by certificated carriers with small aircraft or by helicopter airlines. Of course, this has changed over the years; in fact, as of September 1972, the CAB's definition of "large aircraft" was changed from one with maximum gross takeoff weight exceeding 12,500 pounds to an aircraft having a maximum passenger capacity of more than thirty seats or a maximum payload capacity of more than 7,500 pounds. The 12,500 pounds weight limitation and the limitation as to the markets which air taxis could serve were intended to protect the certificated airlines from competition.[e] In the last several years, under certain circumstances, the CAB allowed a number of commuter airlines to use equipment exceeding the 12,500-pounds limit (usually DC-3s).

During the 1960s, the commuter air-carrier industry experienced tremendous growth as they began serving the markets which were being neglected by the local service airlines who became more interested in serving denser, longer haul markets. In 1960 there were ten scheduled air taxis (or commuter airlines); in April 1972, the National Air Transportation Conferences reported 109 commuter airlines in service. The numbers vary due to the relative instability of the industry, but the facts are that the commuter air carrier industry has undergone a dramatic growth since 1960 and that it is becoming more stable and mature. The CAB reports that during 1972, 168 commuter air carriers registered with the CAB (in one or more quarters),[f] and that during 1973 the number was 180.

The dramatic rise in commuter air firms to provide service to low-population density areas has occurred as a result of the gradual retreat of the large carriers from this type of service.[19] In many low density areas, however, air service can hardly be self-sustaining even at the commuter air carrier level. (Table 2-9 depicts the range of air service available to cities with population less than 100,000 in 1970).[g] The continual reassessment of CAB policy in short-haul air

---

[e]It is interesting to note that the maximum gross takeoff weight of the DC-3 is 25,000 pounds, twice 12,500 pounds. This aircraft was used extensively by the certificated airlines during the 1950s.

[f]During 1971, only 107 commuter air carriers registered for all four quarters. Source: Civil Aeronautics Board, *Commuter Air Carrier Traffic Statistics*, Year Ended December 31, 1971.

[g]The most interesting arrangement in this sector of the industry is between Allegheny Airlines and a group of lessees, who provide air commuter services. The nine Allegheny Commuter operators are the following: AeroMech, Air East, Atlantic City Airlines, Crown Airways, Fischer Brothers Aviation, Henson Aviation, Pocono Airlines, Ransome Airlines, and Vercoa Air Service. The fifteen cities served by these operators are the following: Altoona, Pa.; Atlantic City, N.J.; Danville, Ill.; DuBois, Pa.; Elkins, W. Va.; Franklin, Pa.; Hagerstown, Md.; Hazeltown, Pa.; Johnstown, Pa.; Mansfield, Ohio; Muncie, Ind.; North Philadelphia, Pa.; Salisbury, Md.; Trenton, N.J.; and Wildwood, N.J. In addition to the main hubs, these cities originally were served by Allegheny Airlines and now are served by Allegheny Commuters. For additional background material, see Eads, *Local Service Airline Experiment*, pp. 168-69.

Table 2-9

Air Service at Cities with 1960 Population of Less than 100,000 (Service as of April, 1970)

Service	Number of Cities	Percentage of Total
Trunk Only	11	2.2
Local Only	185	36.3
Commuter Carrier Only	152	29.9
Trunk and Local	30	5.9
Trunk and Commuter	21	4.1
Local and Commuter	89	17.5
Trunk, Local, and Commuter	21	4.1
Total	509	100.0

Source: U.S. Civil Aeronautics Board, Bureau of Operating Rights, *Service to Small Communities*, Part II, March 1972.

service to communities of light traffic density is necessary to bring about a stronger common carrier distribution in the airline industry. The reassessment is important from a policy viewpoint when the users of such service are discovered to be concentrated into a relatively few areas (see Table 2-10).

In examining market structure with respect to particular markets, two broad classifications should be considered: scheduled and nonscheduled service. Sched-

Table 2-10

Commuter Airline Enplaned Passengers in the Eight Busiest Areas, Third Quarter of 1969

Area	Percentage of Total	
Puerto Rico/Virgin Islands	19.1	
Southern California	14.0	41.3
Massachusetts/Maine	8.2	
Houston	4.9	
New York City/Northern New Jersey	4.1	
Chicago	3.1	
Southern Florida	2.9	
Hawaii	2.3	
Others	41.4	

Source: J.T. Kneafsey and J. Cowley, "Economic Impact of Air Service on Low Density Regions," Working Paper, Department of Civil Engineering, M.I.T., June 1973, p. 67.

uled service is that available to the public at a fixed price and according to a published timetable or at sufficiently regular times as to constitute a systematic service. Nonscheduled service refers to the remainder of domestic air service: in effect, charter operations. Airline firms which offer charter service are tenderly referred to as "supplementals." One might ask: Why bother to study the supplemental air carriers? The whole supplemental industry accounts for only 7 percent of the airline industry's annual gross revenue and is not quite as large as Northwest, the seventh largest trunk airline. The supplementals are dismissed as insignificant in some studies because the authors feel, for the most part correctly, that excluding about 20 percent of the industry (supplementals, all cargo air carriers, and air-taxi operations) will not impair their conclusions.[20] Indeed, these carriers operate differently and might distort the results of certain studies, but these differences, especially those of the supplementals, should not be brushed aside so easily. Despite the uncertainty of their existence, the supplementals have proved not only tenacious but have grown over the past decade. Table 2-11 briefly describes some of the characteristics of this section of the industry. The supplementals are mentioned here as an important segment of the industry, even though most of their operations are international in scope.[21]

Urban Transit

A completely separate "industry" exists in the case of urban public transit.[22] This industry includes those activities which support the movement of people in and around an urban area (conventionally denoted as an SMSA or Standard Metropolitan Statistical Area), including: taxicabs, buses, streetcars, trolley coaches, and commuter rail operations. While the data for this industry are difficult to collect, preliminary indications suggest that revenues from this industry, which excludes auto travel, easily exceed 4 billion dollars annually (see Table 2-12). Since most operations in the urban transit industry are conducted by public agencies, an analysis of its characteristics lies beyond the scope of this book.

Comments on Measures of Market Structure

High market concentration and relatively rapid technological change[h] have characterized the following domestic industries: aerospace, aircraft manufacturing, electrical equipment, communications, chemicals, machinery, instruments, and motor vehicles. Casual observations also suggest that a large percentage of the total research and development expenditures in the industrial sector is accounted for by these few industries. These observations then have become the

---

[h]This phrase assumes some capability of empirical measurement.

Table 2-11
Supplemental Air Carriers

Airline[a] (Base City)	Commercial Area Authority[b]	Special Characteristics[c]
Trans International Airlines (Oakland, Calif.)	Transatlantic, Transpacific, Central & South America, Caribbean	Global charters, ITC, Military
Overseas National Airways (New York City	Transatlantic, Caribbean	Concentrated in North Atlantic, Quicktrans, Logair
World Airways (Oakland, Calif.)	Transatlantic, Transpacific, Central & South America, Caribbean	Mainly international charters, Logair; has own maintenance base
Universal Airlines (Ypsilanti, Mich.)	Canada, Mexico	Cargo specialist, automotive cargo, Quicktrans, Logair
Capitol Airways (Nashville, Tenn.; operating base: Wilmington, Del.)	Transatlantic Caribbean	North Atlantic passengers, Logair; has own maintenance base
Saturn Airways (Oakland, Calif.)	Transatlantic Caribbean	Cargo, Logair, North Atlantic passengers, Military charters
American Flyers Airline (Ardmore, Okla.)	Transatlantic, Carribean, Canada, Mexico	Mainly North Atlantic, ITC
Modern Air Transport (Miami, Fla.)	Canada, Mexico (Europe)	N.Y.-Fla. (land buyers), Mexico, ITC, Intra-Europe, Special charters
Southern Air Transport	Caribbean Transpacific	Cargo and livestock
Purdue Airlines (Lafayette, Ind.)	Canada	Special fixed base operator
McCulloch International Airlines (formerly Vance International airways) (Los Angeles)	Canada, Mexico	Fixed base operator
Johnson Flying Service (Missoula, Mont.)	Canada	Fixed base operator, Government forestry contracts

[a]Airlines ranked by 1970 gross revenue.

[b]All airlines have domestic and Hawaii civilian authority and worldwide military charter authority.

[c]Quicktrans and Logair are Air Force and Navy scheduled charter freight operations.

basis for a popularly accepted thesis that large firms in market structures of high concentration are necessary to produce significant progress in technology. The most historically quoted versions of this thesis are by Schumpeter and Galbraith.[23]

The relative importance of the elements of market structure is a matter of

Table 2-12
Selected Urban Transportation Statistics for 1970

| | All Modes | Taxi | Bus, Rail, and Trolley Coach | | | | Commuter Rail[b] |
			Total	Bus	Rail[a]	Trolley Coach	
Revenue Passengers (Millions)	8,660	2,378	5,932	4,058	1,746	128	250
Percentage of all-mode total	100.0	27.8	69.3	47.4	20.4	1.5	2.9
Passenger Revenue (Millions of $'s)	4,070	2,221	1,639	1,194	415	30	210
Percentage of all-mode total	100.0	54.5	40.3	29.4	10.2	0.7	5.1

[a]Includes elevated and subway rail rapid transit, grade-separated surface rail, and streetcar operations.

[b]Urban passenger rail service provided by railroad companies.

Sources: For bus, rail, and trolley coach data: American Transit Association, *1970-71 Transit Fact Book*; for taxicab data: International Taxicab Association; American Automobile Association; and for commuter rail: Interstate Commerce Commission; Boston and Maine Railroad reports.

debate, although there appears to be a consensus that concentration is probably the most basic single determinant.[24] It is certainly regarded as the most adequately measured element, whereas incomplete empirical information accompanies the others. Even with concentration measures, certain problems exist:

It may be true that high concentration ratios are good indicia of the absence of pure competition, but the converse is not true. That is, it may be incorrect to assume that as the number of firms increases, interdependence tends to disappear and that rivalry approaches the structural—and the performance—characteristics of pure competition or the large-number case of monopolistic competition. Low concentration ratios give little assurance that a more complex form of oligopoly does not prevail among the firms.[25]

While an important characteristic of market structure relates to the size of the firms in an industry, a more interesting question, and one which links industrial performance with structure, is whether firms of a given size are more efficient in producing innovative ideas. An even more relevant issue is whether economies of scale result from the full multistage process which consists of generating an innovative idea, developing the innovation, and marketing the resulting output.[26] Some statistical evidence suggests that success in the innovative process is not independent of a firm's size. One study indicates large firms apply new techniques (for a selected group of inventions) more rapidly than small ones.[27] There is also statistical support for the view that volume of sales per unit of research effort is greater for large firms than for small.[28] Despite the empirical evidence for these propositions, the connection between a firm's size and its rate of innovation remains obscure because other studies suggest that smaller firms may be as likely to undertake expenditures on research as large firms (in terms of R & D expense per unit of sales) and that their use of research resources may be no less productive than those of large firms.[29] In addition, many major inventions allegedly have originated in small producing firms rather than large ones.[30]

Economic theory historically has tended to sidestep issues of differences of firm size within industries and changes in market structure.[31] Traditional theory has attempted to explain the phenomenon of increased concentration of industries in terms of technical, managerial, marketing, and financial factors that affected existing firms and industries. Only recently have significant efforts occurred toward explaining the emergence and growth of new firms—and especially the importance of smaller firms.[32] The substantive conclusions from these empirical studies of market structure are relevant to the transportation industries, especially when changes in market structure contemplated by transportation firms are presented to the regulatory agencies for review.

Notes

1. For a statement of this belief, see the classic book by John R. Meyer, Merton S. Peck, John Stenason, and Charles Zwick, *The Economics of Competition in the Transportation Industries* (Cambridge: Harvard University Press, 1959), p. 203.

2. M.A. Adelman, "The Relations between Market Structure and Technology," paper prepared for the Twentieth Century Fund Tocqueville Project, processed, December 1967, p. 10.

3. Ibid., p. 30.

4. In addition, the *1967 Census of Manufacturers* classified the output of all manufacturing establishments into 417 industries. The two-digit Standard Industrial Classification (SIC) code for transport is 37, for aircraft production it is 372, and so on. Complete *Census of Manufacturers* were published in 1947, 1954, 1958, 1963 and 1967. Also a separate *Census of Transportation* was published in 1963 by the Bureau of the Census.

5. Joe S. Bain, *Industrial Organization*, 2nd ed. (New York: John Wiley & Sons, 1968), p. 9.

6. For a thorough review of the literature to date, see John M. Vernon, *Market Structure and Industrial Performance: A Review of Statistical Findings* (Boston: Allyn and Bacon, Inc., 1972).

7. Joe S. Bain, *Barriers to New Competition* (Cambridge: Harvard University Press, 1956), pp. 10-11.

8. Bain, *Industrial Organization*, p. 12.

9. Traditional books in transportation economics tend to examine trans-

portation from an institutional perspective. See, for example, D. Philip Locklin, *Economics of Transportation*, 7th ed. (Homewood, Ill.: Richard D. Irwin, Inc., 1971); Hugh S. Norton, *Modern Transportation Economics*, 2nd ed. (Columbus, Ohio: Charles E. Merrill Books, Inc., 1971); Dudley F. Pegrum, *Transportation: Economics and Public Policy*, rev. ed. (Homewood, Ill.: Richard D. Irwin, Inc., 1968); and a more elementary text by Roy J. Sampson and Martin T. Farris, *Domestic Transportation: Practice, Theory and Policy*, 2nd ed. (Boston: Houghton Mifflin Co., 1971).

10. William G. Shepherd, "Structure and Behavior in British Industries, with U.S. Comparisons," *The Journal of Industrial Economics* 21 (November 1971), p. 35.

11. See Zvi Griliches, "Cost Allocation in Railroad Regulation," *The Bell Journal of Economics and Management Science* 3 (Spring 1972), pp. 26-41.

12. See Charles F. Phillips, Jr., *The Economics of Regulation*, rev. ed. (Homewood, Ill.: Richard D. Irwin, 1969), pp. 484-85.

13. A recent statement of this imputation appears in John C. Spychalski, "Imperfections in Railway Line Abandonment Regulation and Suggestions for Their Correction," *I.C.C. Practitioners' Journal* 40 (May-June 1973), pp. 454-69.

14. See J.T. Kneafsey and M.E. Edelman, "A Market-Oriented Solution to the Northeast Railroad Dilemma," *I.C.C. Practitioners' Journal* (forthcoming).

15. See "Trucking Industry Largest Nixon Donor," *New York Times*, November 7, 1973, p. 34. This article depicts the industry as the largest contributor to the 1972 Nixon campaign by virtue of its legal solicitation of company contributions which totaled $600,000.

16. Almarin Phillips, *Technology and Market Structure: A Study of the Aircraft Industry*, (Lexington, Mass.: Lexington Books, D.C. Heath and Co., 1971), Appendix A, pp. 133-37.

17. George C. Eads, *The Local Service Airline Experiment* (Washington: The Brookings Institution, 1972).

18. Ibid., pp. 3-4.

19. See Virgil D. Cover, "The Rise of Third Level Air Carriers," *Transportation Journal* 11 (Fall 1971), pp. 41-51.

20. See Richard E. Caves, *Air Transport and Its Regulators: An Industry Study* (Cambridge, Mass.: Harvard University Press, 1962); and William A. Jordan, *Airline Regulation in America: Effects and Imperfections* (Baltimore, Md.: The Johns Hopkins University Press, 1970).

21. See Mahlon R. Straszheim, *The International Airline Industry* (Washington: The Brookings Institution, 1969), esp. pp. 217-19.

22. See Institute for Defense Analyses, *Economic Characteristics of the Urban Public Transportation Industry*, prepared for the U.S. Department of Transportation (Washington: U.S. Government Printing Office, February 1972).

23. See Joseph A. Schumpeter, *Capitalism, Socialism and Democracy* (New York: Harper and Row, 1950); and J.K. Galbraith, *American Capitalism, The Concept of Countervailing Power* (Cambridge, Mass.: Riverside Press, 1952).

24. See William Shepherd, *Market Power and Economic Welfare: An Introduction* (New York: Random House, 1970).

25. Almarin Phillips, *Market Structure, Organization and Performance* (Cambridge, Mass.: Harvard University Press, 1962), p. 23.

26. See R. Vernon, "Organization as A Scale Factor in the Growth of Firms," in J. Markshak and G. Papanek, *Industrial Organization and Economic Development: In Honor of E.S. Mason* (Boston: Houghton-Mifflin Co., 1970), pp. 47-66.

27. See Edwin Mansfield, "The Speed of Response of Firms to New Techniques," *Quarterly Journal of Economics* 77 (May 1963), pp. 290-311.

28. See F.M. Scherer, "Firm Size and Patented Inventions." *American Economic Review* 55 (December 1965), pp. 1097-1123.

29. See Daniel Hamberg, *R&D, Essays on the Economics of Research and Development* (New York: Random House, 1966); and W.S. Comanor, "Market Structure, Product Differentiation, and Industrial Research," *Quarterly Journal of Economics* 81 (November 1967), pp. 639-57.

30. See especially Edwin Mansfield, *The Economics of Technological Change* (New York: W.W. Norton and Co., 1968), pp. 107-110; his companion volume is entitled: *The Economics of Research and Development* (New York: W.W. Norton and Co., 1968); and J. Jewkes, D. Sawers, and R. Stillerman, *The Sources of Invention* (New York: St. Martin's Press, 1958).

31. Alfred Marshall's classic treatment in his *Principles of Economics* (London: MacMillan, 8th ed., reprinted 1966) of the "representative firm," intended particularly to handle industries with decreasing costs, as a case in point.

32. See David Waite, "The Economic Significance of Small Firms," *The Journal of Industrial Economics* 21 (April 1973), pp. 154-65.

3 Industrial Performance in Transportation

A general methodological approach to the economic analysis of markets is often referred to as market structure analysis.[1] From the discussion in Chapter 2, this approach is based on three principal concepts: structure, conduct, and performance. Although the general flow of causation is from structure to conduct to performance, there are exceptions which will be discussed later. For the present analysis, however, it is only necessary to stress the one-way direction of causation from market structure to industrial performance.

The Use of Economic Theory

The basic hypotheses and notions of standards for industrial performance can be obtained from the abstract world of economic theory. It is necessary to examine the concepts of structure and performance in this abstract world as a precondition to evaluating the public policy issues of industrial organization. Thus the purpose of this chapter is to analyze the fundamentals of the economic theory of markets and to provide a linkage between this theory and various empirical studies of market structure. These fundamentals include brief discussions of the economic models of competition and monopoly and their performance implications. While these two models represent extreme cases, there may be individual markets in transportation which conform to their characteristics. It is much more probable, though, that transportation firms operate in monopoly markets than in perfectly competitive ones. Even more probable is that transportation firms participate in imperfectly competitive markets, like monopolistic competition and a variety of oligopolies. Thus some of these imperfectly competitive markets with variations on the profit maximization objective, which is the heart of the theory of the firm, will be examined.

Perfect Competition

This market structure consists of firms producing an item Z and selling this product in a market characterized by: (1) product homogeneity, (2) many firms, (3) many consumers, (4) freedom of entry, (5) perfect information, and (6) no collusion. The market price P for the competitive firm's product is determined by the intersection of the market demand function and the market supply function. The firm's total cost function is given by

37

$$C = f(Z) \tag{3.1}$$

The firm's profit π is by definition equal to the difference between total revenue TR and total cost C:

$$\pi = TR - C \tag{3.2}$$

$$= P \cdot Z - f(Z) \tag{3.3}$$

Total profit is maximized when the derivative of profit with respect to output is equal to zero:

$$\frac{d\pi}{dZ} = P - \frac{d(C)}{dZ} = 0 \tag{3.4}$$

or when marginal cost MC is equal to price:

$$MC = P \tag{3.5}$$

which graphically will hold when the slope of the firm's total cost function is equal to the slope of the total revenue function. In Figure 3-1, total profit (ST)

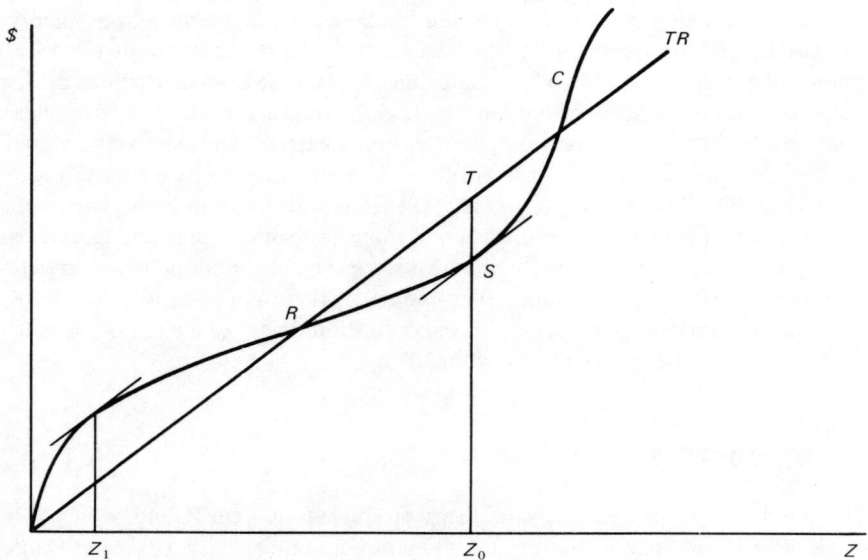

Figure 3-1. Profit Maximization for the Competitive Firm

is at a maximum at output Z_o, when the vertical distance between TR and C is a maximum. In examining Figure 3-1, note that MC also equals P at output Z_1 but total profit is clearly not at a maximum.[a]

In the short run, when the firm cannot vary its fixed factors of production, it will have no incentive to change its rate of output from the level at which $MC = P$. Total profit will decrease when output is either increased above Z_0 or decreased below Z_0 in Figure 3-1. Hence, the firm is said to be in short-run equilibrium when output is such that $MC = P$. Figure 3-2 suggests an important

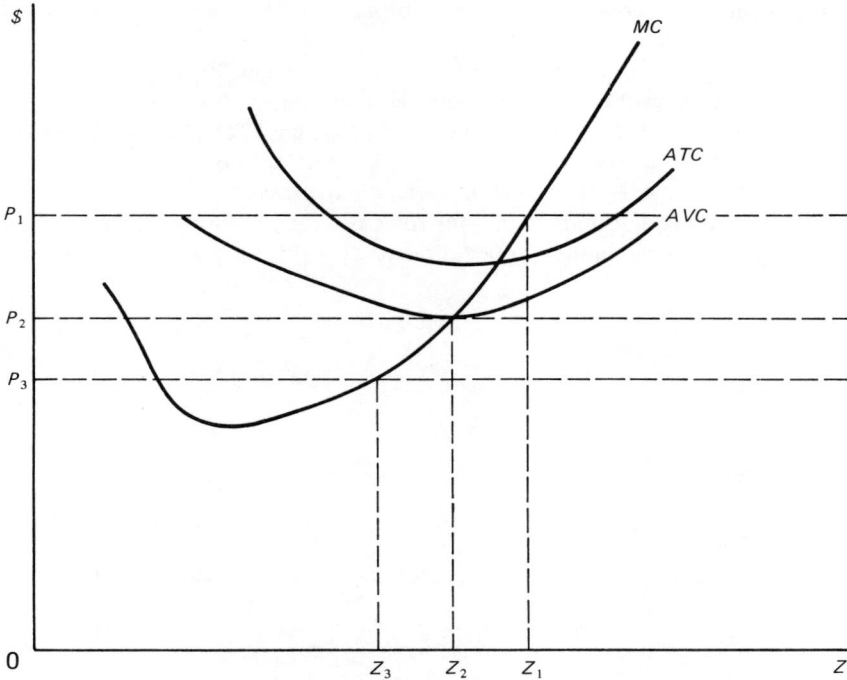

Figure 3-2. Short-Run Equilibrium for the Competitive Firm

[a]In fact, total profit is negative and at a minimum at output Z_1. To guarantee that total profit is maximized when $MC = P$, the second derivative of profit must be negative:

$$\frac{d^2\pi}{dZ^2} = \frac{-d^2C}{dZ^2} < 0$$

or

$$\frac{d(MC)}{dZ} < 0$$

limitation to the profit-maximization rule: if price falls below average variable cost, AVC, the firm's profit will be greater (or its loss will be less) if it produces no output at all than if it produces a positive output.

The short-run supply function for a competitive industry is simply the lateral sum of the short-run supply functions for all of the firms in the industry. Since the short-run supply function of each firm in the industry has a positive slope, it follows that the industry short-run supply function is fixed. This is attributable to two factors: first, the supply functions (MC functions) of all of the firms in the industry are fixed in the short run; and second, in the short run there are not sufficient time and opportunity for new firms to enter, or for existing firms to leave, the industry.

In the long run, all factors of production are variable. Figure 3-3 shows the long-run marginal cost curve (MC) and the average total cost curve (ATC) for a typical firm in a competitive industry. Both MC and ATC are derived from the firm's long-run total cost function, and since there are no fixed factors in the long run, average total cost is equal to average variable cost.

The long-run equilibrium conditions for a perfectly competitive industry are that every firm in the industry maximizes profit ($P = MC$) and that a long-run

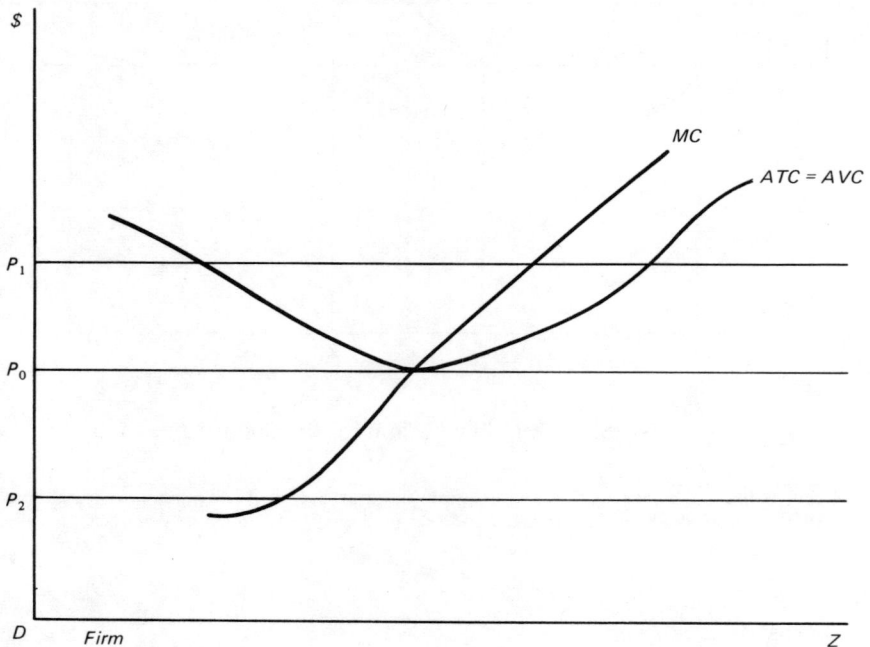

Figure 3-3. Long-Run Equilibrium for a Perfectly Competitive Firm

minimum ATC (including normal profit) for every firm in the industry be just equal to the market price P. If this latter condition does not hold, then firms will either be entering or leaving the industry. Combining the short-run equilibrium condition $P = MC$ with the long-run equilibrium condition $ATC = P$ yields:

$$P = MC = ATC \qquad (3.6)$$

where MC and ATC are now long-run costs rather than short run. The firm's long-run supply function is simply that portion of its increasing long-run MC curve which lies above long-run AVC (which is equal to ATC). If price falls below minimum ATC, than zero output is produced.[b] Since it is an extreme, the model of perfect competition in practice is recognized as an unattainable ideal. Consequently, performance becomes difficult to describe. The most valuable aspect of this market structure, though, resides in its hypothetical foundations.

Monopoly

This market structure has a sole producer of a unique product Z for which there are no close substitutes. Entry to this market is in effect blocked. The demand curve for the monopolist is equivalent to the market demand function in a competitive market since there may be many buyers. Because increases in output can only be achieved by reductions in the price charged by the monopolist, the monopolist cannot sell unlimited quantities of its output at a given price. The demand curve for a monopoly firm may be expressed as

$$P = P(Z) \text{ where } \frac{dP}{dZ} < 0 \qquad (3.7)$$

or

$$AR = AR(Z) \qquad (3.8)$$

where AR denotes average revenue. Total revenue is defined as

$$TR(Z) = P(Z) \cdot Z \qquad (3.9)$$

---

[b]The long-run supply function for the industry is more intricate. An industry characterized by fixed factor prices is called a *constant-cost industry*. An *increasing-cost industry* is one where an increase in the industry's output as a whole may bid up prices of the inputs and/or may cause an unfavorable shift in a firm's production functions, both of which tend to increase the total cost of firms in the industry. A *decreasing-cost industry* is one which increases in output for the industry as a whole lead to favorable technological progress and/or the discovery of cheaper sources of raw materials, both of which tend to reduce the total costs of firms in the industry.

For the monopolist, the necessary condition for profit maximization is that

$$\frac{d\pi}{dZ} = \frac{dTR}{dZ} - \frac{dC}{dZ} = 0 \qquad (3.10)$$

or

$$MR = MC, \qquad (3.11)$$

the equalizing of marginal revenue and marginal costs.[c]

The optimum level of output $\overline{Z}$ for the monopolist can be found by solving equations 3.10 or 3.11 for Z. It is assumed that $AR(\overline{Z}) \geqslant AVC(\overline{Z})$ or otherwise the firm will produce nothing in the short run. The monopolist's optimum selling price $\overline{P}$ can be found by substituting $\overline{Z}$ into equation 3.8. Figure 3-4 illustrates graphically the monopolist's optimum price-output decision.

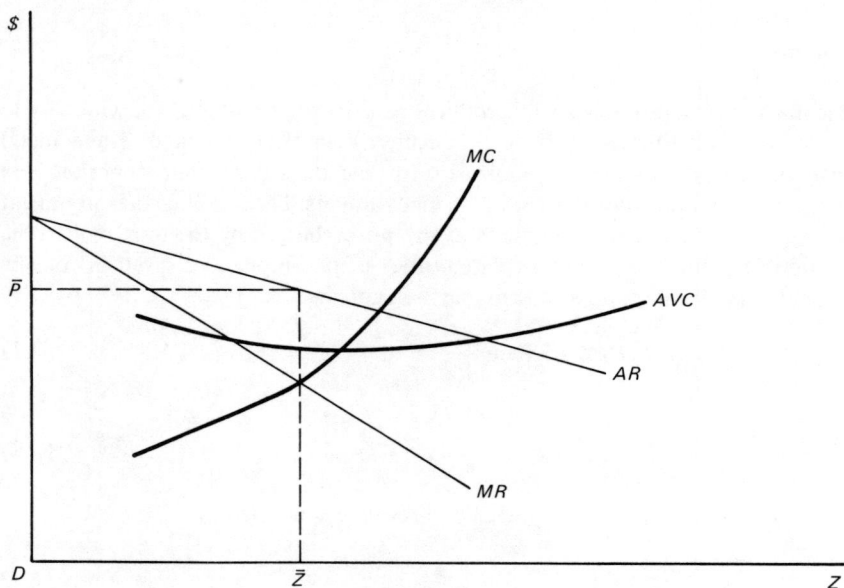

Figure 3-4. The Monopolist's Optimum Price-Output Decision

---

[c]A sufficient condition for profit maximization is that the firm's profit function be strictly concave over all Z. That is, the second derivative of profit with respect to output must be negative:

$$\frac{d^2\pi}{dZ^2} < 0$$

The second derivative of the firm's profit function will be negative if the firm's marginal revenue function is decreasing and if its cost function behaves in a certain prescribed manner.

The preceding analysis of the behavior of the monopolist has been limited to the short run. However, since entry to the industry is blocked, the analysis of a monopolist's behavior in the long run is of limited interest. The only difference between the long-run and short-run monopolist cases is in terms of the possible shapes of the cost function.

The equilibrium output of the monopolist has the important property that price exceeds marginal cost. This divergence is the usual basis for the policy condemnation of monopolies, since a price-marginal cost gap supposedly represents a misallocation of resources by virtue of the restriction of output. The result of this output restriction is that a marginal dollar's worth of resources produces more than a dollar's worth of output (since price exceeds marginal cost) in a monopoly whereas in competition the marginal dollar of resources produces exactly one dollar of output (since price equals marginal cost): the inference being that reallocating resources from competitive industries to monopolies would increase the value of the economy's output. Consequently, performance in the context for monopoly firms is regarded as poor.

Imperfect Competition

Imperfect competition is a term used to describe market situations which lie somewhere between the two extremes of perfect competition and pure monopoly. In the theory of "monopolistic competition," five of the assumptions of perfect competition are retained: (1) many firms, (2) many consumers, (3) freedom of entry, (4) perfect information, and (5) no collusion. The assumption of product homogeneity is dropped: that is, each firm is assumed to offer a produce or service which is differentiated in some way from that of its competitors. This is a situation which most nearly corresponds to the real-world activities of railroads, assuming that a reasonable definition of output is acceptable.

The demand curve for a monopolistically competitive firm has a negative slope, with the managers of a typical firm assumed to behave as though their actions had no effect on the behavior of competitors. In the short run, firms will maximize profit by maintaining an output level at which MC equals MR. This condition is necessary and sufficient for profit maximization if the firm's marginal profit function is decreasing, as was the case with a monopoly. With freedom of entry, as under perfect competition, both profits and losses will approach zero in the long run: That is,

$$AR = ATC \tag{3.12}$$

Figure 3-5 shows graphically the long-run equilibrium position of the monopolistically competitive firm. At output level $\overline{Z}, MR = MC$ and $AR = ATC$ with the

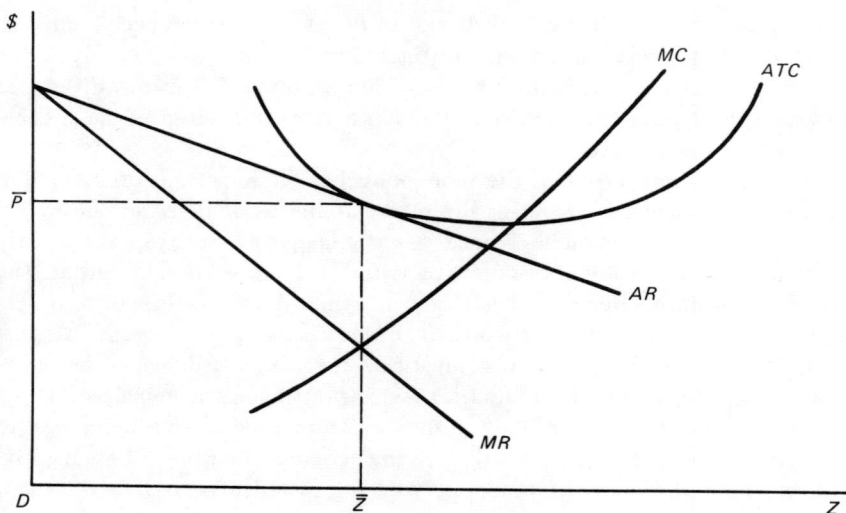

Figure 3-5. Long-Run Equilibrium for a Firm under Monopolistic Competition

equilibrium price of P. Note that the point of tangency between AR and ATC lies above minimum ATC.[d]

Various statistical attempts have been made to estimate directly the social losses caused by monopolistic resource allocation.[2] Although a detailed discussion of these studies is not warranted here, a brief explanation of the theory which underlies the studies should be helpful. The statistical studies were essentially directed toward estimating the "deadweight welfare loss" associated with the restriction of output by monopoly elements. These restrictions can take many forms and can affect any industry. In the transportation industries, one form of output restriction may occur as a result of rate regulation, especially if rates are inflexibly set higher than competitive rates which would otherwise prevail. The predictable outcome of such a rate regulatory policy would be lower-than-competitive equilibrium output.

Welfare Loss Due to Monopoly

This section describes the effects of the imposition of regulatory restrictions on the economy from the point of view of both consumers and producers. One form of regulatory restriction is the imposition of fixed rates for the shipments of commodities. This section is segmented into three areas:

---

[d]It is easy to demonstrate mathematically that the long-run marginal cost curve in Figure 3-5 intersects MR at the same output level Z for which AR is tangent to ATC.

1. Consumer response to rate changes
2. The calculation of the deadweight loss to society
3. Impacts by income group

The response of final consumers to the manner in which transportation rates are changed (or not changed as the case might be) and thereby affecting product prices is a predictable process. This process is depicted in Figure 3-6, which indicates the more detailed interrelationships among the above three areas. Once the shifts in cost per ton-km for any carrier are known or estimated (regardless of the cause), rate changes can be posted which in effect shift the prices per ton by commodity class. The process by which rate (tariff) changes are implemented in the economy is considered exogenous to this example, although in some cases the mere announcement effect of a rate change resulting from a cost shift may evoke quick consumer response. It is also assumed that producers are profit maximizers who operate in the best interests of their firms.

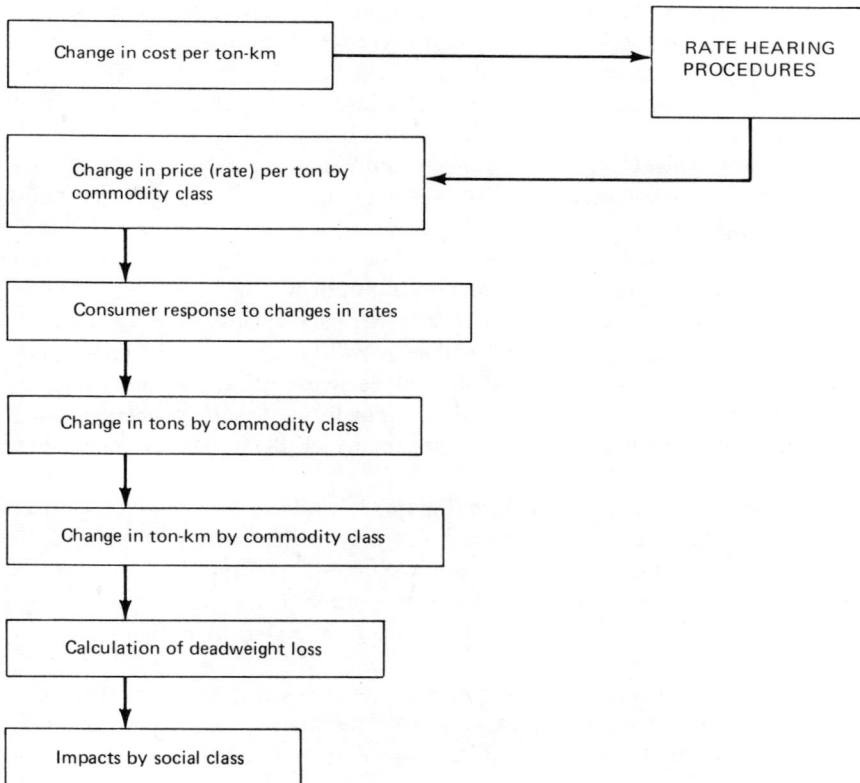

```
┌─────────────────────────────┐                      ┌──────────────────┐
│ Change in cost per ton-km   │─────────────────────→│ RATE HEARING     │
└─────────────────────────────┘                      │ PROCEDURES       │
                                                      └──────────────────┘
┌─────────────────────────────┐                              │
│ Change in price (rate) per  │←─────────────────────────────┘
│ ton by commodity class      │
└─────────────────────────────┘
              │
              ▼
┌─────────────────────────────┐
│ Consumer response to        │
│ changes in rates            │
└─────────────────────────────┘
              │
              ▼
┌─────────────────────────────┐
│ Change in tons by           │
│ commodity class             │
└─────────────────────────────┘
              │
              ▼
┌─────────────────────────────┐
│ Change in ton-km by         │
│ commodity class             │
└─────────────────────────────┘
              │
              ▼
┌─────────────────────────────┐
│ Calculation of deadweight   │
│ loss                        │
└─────────────────────────────┘
              │
              ▼
┌─────────────────────────────┐
│ Impacts by social class     │
└─────────────────────────────┘
```

Figure 3-6. Effects of Changes in Carrier Operating Costs on Consumers

Consumer Response to Rate Changes

The extent to which consumers react to the changes in rates affects directly the amount of tons shipped by commodity class, which in turn affects the volume of ton-km shipped by commodity class for the nation as a whole. Given the fact that both rates and volumes (output) will change and that relevant data are available, any regulatory commission should be in a better position to examine the social impacts of a particular factor invoking these changes.

The Deadweight Loss Associated
with the Imposition of Rate Regulation

Although estimations of this type contain some error and are subject to qualification, it is possible to approximate the social costs of restrictions on fluctuating rates for the motor trucking industry. This can be done by calculating what is known as the deadweight loss associated with market interferences and subsequently with less-than-competitive pricing. Since the net effect of imposing tariff restrictions (rate regulation) may be to force some operators out of the market, the trucking industry might eventually consist of fewer participants than would be the case without any regulation.[e]

In a purely competitive market (or one approximating such conditions), the supply curve represents marginal cost and each quoted rate should necessarily equal marginal cost. If trucking firms offer only the transport of each commodity at marginal cost plus some markup (to account for adjustments as a result of new posted rates), the equilibrium output will fall. The result will be that consumers will be worse off while the remaining trucking firms (producers) will be better off. Since the producers' gains will fail to offset the consumers' losses, however, the nation as a whole will be worse off as a result of pricing policies which become somewhat less than competitive. This phenomenon is said to create a deadweight loss to the nation for which there is no countervailing compensation.

These issues can be depicted in Figure 3-7, which shows a competitive equilibrium (assume that this is the case in which market forces determine rates) where the prevailing rate (price) is P^* and the prevailing output is X^*. As long as the industry has unrestricted participants, the supply curve, SS_0, represents the summation of each trucker's marginal cost curve whereby price equals marginal cost (at B).

Now suppose that rate regulation policies are imposed. This means that some producers (truckers) will be squeezed out of the market and others will face additional costs (perhaps a markup) on top of their prior marginal costs. The

---

[e]This outcome would also occur under other forms of market structure barriers, like a standard axle weight restriction policy or uniform maintenance requirements.

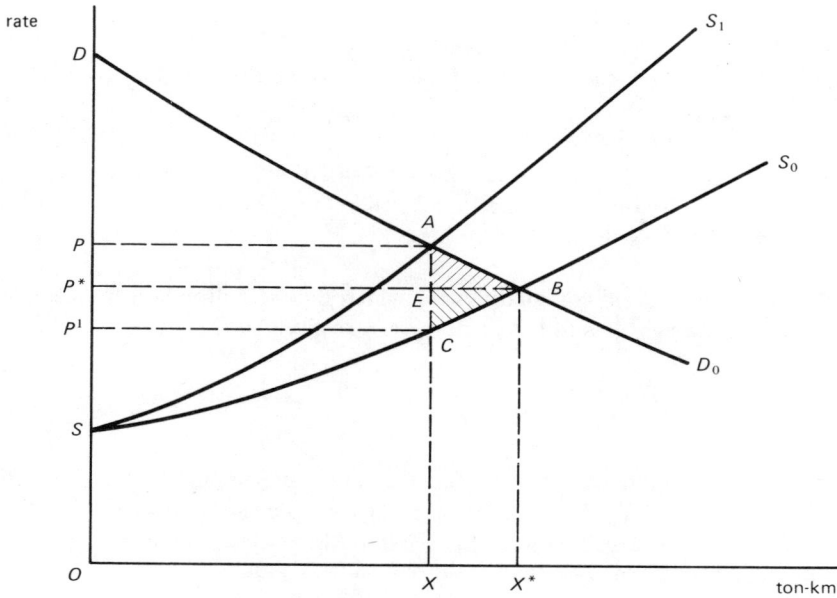

Figure 3-7. A Graphical Analysis of the Deadweight Loss

result is that the supply curve is effectively raised to SS_1 with equilibrium rates rising to P and equilibrium output falling to X.

The loss in consumer surplus is depicted by the area $PP*BA$, but the gain in producer surplus is less than the loss, since area AEB is lost from the consumer's side and area EBC is lost from the producer's side. The total loss therefore is the area ABC, which represents a deadweight loss to the nation for which there is no compensation and which would occur when the regulation of rates in excess of competitive prices is imposed. Admittedly, the loss may be small in percentage terms, but it can be substantial in absolute monetary units.

As long as the demand and supply functions are linear over the relevant range, the deadweight loss associated with rate regulation (or monopoly pricing) can be determined by the following formula:

$$L = \frac{1}{2}\Delta P\Delta X$$

where ΔP is the divergence between the actual rate and the marginal cost p' at

volume (output) X^*,
ΔX is the divergence between the output (without rate regulation) X^* and the output (with rate regulation) X, and L in effect equals the area of the triangle ABC or the deadweight loss.

By summing over all commodities for which the rates diverge from marginal costs, the deadweight loss to the economy can be given by

$$L = \frac{1}{2}\sum_i \Delta P_i \Delta X_i$$

where ΔP_i is the divergence between the rate and marginal cost for the ith commodity, and ΔX_i is the divergence between pre- and postrate regulation output. For superior estimation, this relationship can be manipulated to yield additional information, such that

$$\frac{L}{\sum P_i X_i} = \frac{1}{2}\sum_i Z_i \partial_i \epsilon_i$$

where $\sum_i P_i X_i$ = total ton-km,

Z_i = the share of total output (ton-km) produced by commodity type i,

∂_i = the ratio of the divergence between the rate and marginal cost to rate for commodity type i, $(\frac{\text{rate-marginal cost}}{\text{rate}})_i$, and

ϵ_i = elasticity of demand for the ith commodity.

The expression gives the deadweight loss as a proportion of the output of the trucking industry. Once the deadweight loss is determined, this amount can be used as a gauge to estimate the irrecoverable losses to the economy as a result of imposing a rate regulation policy on motor carriers. The analysis can be extended further to the railroad, airline, and other regulated industries. It must be remembered, though, that this approach to estimating the losses is extremely partial and does not take into account all the interactions within the economy. Nevertheless, it does provide some idea about the magnitude of the policy from which regulatory commissions can assess the impacts of these actions on the economy.

The formula can be used in a fairly straightforward fashion to estimate the misallocative losses, assuming that the share of total traffic (Z_i), the elasticities (ϵ_i), and the divergences from marginal costs (∂_i) are known for each commodity group. In the United States, data for Z_i and ∂_i are provided by the Interstate Commerce Commission and can be computed quite easily. Data on elasticities, however, are less reliable but are available and can be calculated by regulatory commissions for, at minimum, a cluster of commodities, say exports, grains, imports, and domestic commodities. An example of how some sample estimates could be developed is presented in Table 3-1.

The example in Table 3-1 implies that the deadweight loss attributed to imposing rate restrictions is on the order of 3.01 percent of all truck revenues. If these annual revenues were 6 billion dollars, then the welfare losses would be about 200 million dollars. This loss represents the deadweight loss to the economy as a result of rate regulatory policy. It must be stressed that these losses are quite gross and may overestimate the welfare losses in some respects and underestimate them in others.

Impacts by Income Group

Since motor trucking is an intermediate good, the distortions and misallocations existing in the transportation sector will be magnified in other sectors. To the extent that a deadweight loss occurs, a rate regulation policy should also lead to distortions on consumption and income. These distortions can be traced out as incomes "lost" by the nation as a whole and by the various income classifica-

Table 3-1
An Example of Calculating the Deadweight Loss

Commodity Group	Proportion of Total Revenue	Ratio of Deviation from Optimal Price to New Rate	Absolute Value of Elasticity of Demand	Deadweight Loss as Proportion of Revenue[a]
Meats	0.08	0.10	0.6	0.00048
Grains	0.15	0.15	0.5	0.0008
Processed Foods	0.10	0.20	0.8	0.0032
Manufactured Goods	0.22	.	0.9	–
Mining Products	.	.	0.5	–
.	.	.	.	
.	.	.	.	
.	.	.	.	
All Commodities	1.00	–	–	0.0301

[a]Let $L = 0.5\,(Z_i\,\partial_i^2\,\epsilon_i)$

tions as segregated in the existing Bureau of the Census data. If the effect of a rate regulation policy is a priori regressive with respect to tax incidence, the burden of this deadweight loss would fall most heavily on the lower income groups. While these estimates may be subject to significant errors, they nonetheless represent large magnitudes and should not be ignored.

Problems in the Measurement of Transportation Performance

Efforts at devising measures of transportation performance are certainly not new. Such measures have been available for a very long time and are used as a matter of course by a wide variety of individuals and organizations concerned with transportation. While everyone in the transportation field is certainly familiar with measures such as ton-miles, vehicle-miles, and passenger-miles, it is significant to note that frequently the data and constructs used to measure transportation performance have been the by-product of administrative and reporting systems.

On the output side, most analysts agree that virtually no single measure will suffice. In the theoretical literature on the subject, the fundamental distinctions go no farther than indicating that output may reflect either (1) an annual volume; or (2) a rate of output; or (3) a size grouping or batch of output.[3] In fact, even this type of distinction may be the exception to the rule.[4]

One of the earlier attempts to review the literature and to identify the "proper" amount of measurement for transportation output was provided by Wilson, who argued that the sales unit, the ton-mile, is the most appropriate.[5] The problem of measurement arises primarily because firms offer from the supply side vehicle journeys whereas they sell their services in units of ton-miles. Wilson's argument is based on the assumption that the ton-mile is the more properly construed service. A more recent article suggests that the only reason that transport-sales have come to be measured in ton-miles is that existing regulatory policy has deemed it so.[6] The more recent view suggests that changes should be geared for the use of equipment (that is, the supply side) and not its contents. This approach is a call for capacity-oriented transport pricing, for example, unit-trains, containerization, and rent-a-train. While there are other precedents for this form of pricing[7] (and even though some of these have occurred under regulatory policy), it is apparent that competitive incentives yield sales units that indeed do differ from the ton-mile, as suggested in the article by Olson and Brown:

Recognition of an output unit that reflects competitive conditions in transportation would do much toward putting to rest the meaningless controversy that has resulted from defining the output unit in terms of the ton-mile.[8]

Even though some agreement might be reached on the appropriate output unit, it still cannot encompass several other important dimensions which are implicit in measuring output. Some of these other dimensions include:

1. The difference between moving an object through a high impedence as opposed to a low impedence medium
2. The value, or the utility, to the beneficiary of the object movement
3. The importance of accessibility changes induced by both for actual or potential object movement
4. The (potentially movable) objects not moved because of transportation considerations (e.g., communication substituted for transportation)
5. The many public policy uses of transportation output measures[9]

On the input side, the major problem appears to stem from the collection of data. In many cases of transportation and economic modeling, inputs can be specified very appealingly. Quite often, however, the data to support these inputs are either lacking or impossible to collect.

The difficulties of measurement relating to outputs and inputs present more than analytical issues. They also have important practical implications in the area of cost allocation. If transportation systems require rates to reflect costs, then a precise knowledge of the unit to be costed is necessary so that no distortions in the rate making process arise. Otherwise, discrepancies between costs and rates will be sustained and resource misallocation in transportation will continue.

Data Requirements for Railroad
Freight Operations

The bulk of data on rail freight operations has been collected and published by the Interstate Commerce Commission since 1892. The basic reporting mechanism is the annual *Form A* document, from which virtually every secondary statistic is derived. Each Class I railroad (with annual operating revenues in excess of $5 million) must report its balance sheet and income statement items in this document. The level of detail is overwhelming and covers a very large, though diminishing, number of categories. In most cases, however, the data are not very useful.

The uninitiated observer might ask: Why is there this paradox of a potentially rich data set which is not very reliable? The answer lies simply in the problem of the reporting mechanism, for railroad companies keep at least five sets of records:

1. Records for the *Form A* documents which must be completed annually by statutory requirement

2. Records to be furnished stockholders, investment houses, commercial banks, and the financial community: a more limited data set, which is selective in highlighting certain accounts and does not necessarily conform with the *Form A* figures
3. Reports to the Securities and Exchange Commission (SEC) which are ostensibly the same as the stockholders' report, but rarely are; this one is much more detailed and informative, whereas the stockholders' report is "massaged" and selective
4. Company Division reports, which reflect more disaggregate data and are designed to show performance levels of different divisions within a railroad and which represent the best known and realistically available source of information (although in all cases, they are proprietary since they are an internal source)
5. Company Management reports, available only to those few who really know about the true position of the company on a daily basis (it need not be the top management personnel)

Obviously, data set (5.) should remain within the confines of management unless the company is reporting false or fraudulent information. The key data source then is (4.): if these records were more generally available, the empirical merits of railroad industry data (especially for performance) would be enhanced severalfold.

A significant step in this direction occurred with the active participation of the Southern Railway System in providing internal information to an MIT research project under FRA sponsorship (this project is discussed in Chapter 4, note *m*). As soon as other railroads realize that a more widespread exposure of their operations is constructive, the entire empirical world will benefit. At this time, the transportation analyst has only the published sources at his disposal. Internal sources clearly offer the more promising avenue, although their availability is not an immediate possibility. In the interim, one must innovate and use combinations of data sources. The remainder of this section deals with some of these sources.

The traditional method for diagnosing areas of competition in the transportation industries is to compare the cost functions of competing modes for given blocks of traffic. This method tends to equate the similarities in cost levels with the intensity of competition. The classic example of this approach is the Meyer, et al. treatise, *The Economics of Competition in the Transportation Industries.*[10] The difficulty with this approach is that it requires data to be accurate and truly representative of the cost categories to which they relate.

More recent evidence concerning the competition between rail and trucking suggests that only a small percentage of traffic is truly noncompetitive (and only for a limited number of commodities).[11] If this evidence is correct, and if one mode wishes to at least maintain its market share, then either of two events must occur: (1) commodity traffic must be diverted from one mode to the other; or (2) one mode must generate growth of its respective commodity volume more rapidly than the other.

In most cases, it appears that neither railroads nor trucking firms have access to the types of data on commodity movements which they need as a basis for estimating commodity growth rates, elasticities, and market trends. Some types of data have been collected over a period of time, but many of these are poorly designed to handle the problems that are of specific interest to developing service measures.

The *1967 Census of Transportation*[12] contains data on the traffic of manufactured goods and focuses on that class of traffic which is most highly contested by the rail and trucking and is quantitatively most important to both modes. Manufactured items accounted for virtually all the traffic of motor common carriers and for 45 percent of the tonnage and 74 percent of the revenues of the railroads in 1968. A modal split of traffic in manufactured commodities as a function of length of haul demonstrates that, as expected, the rail share grows and trucking shares diminish with increasing distance.[13] The important determinants of modal split and intermodal competition remain obscured in the idiosyncratic traits of shippers and consignees. This aspect can be diagnosed only if more standardized O-D data were available. The kinds of data which should be standardized to use in models describing commodity movements and the performance of railroad firms in hauling those volumes are now described.

Market Shares for Particular Commodity Groups. Market share data, because of their competitive importance and difficulty of collection, are among the most difficult freight data to obtain.[14] The most comprehensive market share data are based on the *1967 Census of Transportation*. These market share estimates differ in the types and levels of aggregation performed on the raw data collected by the Census Bureau. Some of these data for selected commodity groups (2 to 5 digits) are obtained from a public use tape prepared by the Census Bureau and available for a fee from a private firm. The origins and destinations of those market share estimates consist of groups of SMSAs that can be considered to act economically as a single unit. This means that a single origin or destination may contain several counties (the basic SMSA units) and a number of cities. These data represent the most disaggregate data in terms of both commodity and geography that are available from the Census Bureau. Finer levels of detail are prohibited by the deterioration of statistical confidence and the requirements for confidentiality imposed by statute.

Mileage Data. Specific mileage figures are usually required for data sets with specific origins and destinations. The mileage figures can be used in econometric model estimations either directly as internal variables or to calculate other external variables. Since specific mileages have no meaning for data aggregated over the entire United States, the following two variables could be taken from the *1967 Census of Transportation* for use in most data sets:

$M < 200$ = fraction of all tons of a commodity shipped less than 200 straight line miles

$M > 1000$ = fraction of all tons of a commodity shipped more than 1000 straight line miles.

These two variables are suggested because each should correlate strongly with the secure market for each respective mode, as explained above.

Annual Tonnage. Measures of annual traffic volume are often required for the United States as a whole and for specific city and county pairs. The tonnage estimates for the nation again can be taken from the *Census of Transportation*, but estimates for city and county pair tonnages are not generally available.

Value per Ton. The measures of annual tons for the United States as a whole can be used not only as a variable, but often to calculate the value per ton (wholesale) of various commodity groups. To obtain these valuations at the three, four, and five digit STCC levels, the estimates of the total value of shipments made by manufacturers can be divided by the estimates of annual production for the nation.[15] This process is complicated by several factors. First, the *Census of Manufactures* and the *Census of Transportation* do not always agree on the same STCC (SIC) codes at the 5-digit level (see, for example, furniture, STCC 25). Second, the production volume statistics for many commodities in the *Census of Manufactures* are not reported in tons but in some other unit. In such cases, the annual tonnage estimates of the *Census of Transportation* can be used if they are available and considered reliable. Third, the manufacturing statistics on production volumes are primarily reported at the 5- and 7-digit level, requiring aggregation to obtain estimates at the 4- and 3-digit levels. Thus it is not always possible to obtain estimates of both the value and the weight of all shipments of a specific commodity.

To derive estimates of value at the 2-digit level, a different technique can be used. The classification by the ICC in studies on the fractions of rail transport charges in wholesale value of goods can be adapted to match as nearly as possible the 2-digit STCC codes, and the wholesale value for each class can be calculated.[16] These estimates are inconsistent with the former measures in that they are based on prices in 1959 and are biased toward rail-transported commodities. However, limited use is made of 2-digit commodity movements, so these inconsistencies are not serious for most empirical needs.

Rail Freight Rates. The need for rate information for any models employing external factors (SMSA-to-SMSA data) necessitates an estimation of regression equations for rail rates. One would think that more precise rate data could be obtained, but this is not possible.[17] The rate variable that is used in many causal models is the difference between the carload rail rate and the truckload motor rate.[f] This particular differential is used for two reasons: first, a rational shipper should base his mode choice on the difference between rates, and second, the relevant competitive rates should be based on average carload and truckload weights rather than equal weights.[18]

Transit Times. While a proper measure of overall transit time would be the span between the receipt by the carrier of a request for service and the delivery of the shipment to the consignee's loading dock, there are no data available that could provide all this information. Service data collected by railroads usually measure the time from entry of a loaded boxcar into the origin yard to the exit of the boxcar from the destination yard on its way to delivery.[g] Since the time for pick-up and delivery of boxcars is longer than for trailers, there is a bias toward rail if these times are omitted.

It is essential that exact measures of rail transit times be available because estimation of this factor is imprecise at best. It is not essential to have similar data for trucks because truckload-transit times of motor carriers are much more strongly related to route mileage than are rail shipments. A specific requirement would be for rail performance data in the form of trip time distributions for various city pairs or yard pairs for two major railroads. Unfortunately, if there is very little market share data available for one of the railroads in a study, one must concentrate on the network for which performance data are measured on a city-to-city basis. Even this procedure causes two problems: first, the market share data sometimes cover geographic areas not served by the yards for which the performance data are taken, and second, many cities have more than one yard, so unwanted aggregation of performance data may occur. Since the transit time differential between rail and truck is known to be one of the most important factors affecting mode choice, the ability to obtain good estimates of this differential is important. While the data described above are not so exact as desired, they are better than many other approximations used in previous research studies.

Reliability. Obtaining meaningful measures of reliability can be more of a problem than measuring transit time differentials due to the increased impact of aggregation on reliability measures. The main problem arises in the rail data when more than one yard is located in a city. While the mean transit time for both yards is accurately measured by aggregating the movements in or out of

---

[f]Carload and truckload weights and rates are based on regional averages for each commodity.

[g]If a boxcar is put on constructive placement, it is considered "delivered" by the railroad as far as performance measures are concerned. (Constructive placement describes the situation in which a car is ready for delivery but the shipper does not yet want it. The car is then held at the final yard by the railroad until the shipper sends notification that he wants delivery.)

both yards, the same is not necessarily true for reliability measures. For instance, two yards receiving perfectly reliable (zero variance) moves, but with different transit times will appear, upon aggregation, to have substantial variance. However, individual shippers, if receiving cars from only one of the yards, will not perceive any unreliability. It is also uncertain that all shippers served by a single yard obtain the same service reliability because of rail customer preferences, frequency of switch runs, or other reasons. Thus the aggregation of performance data into a single reliability measure could be very misleading.

Because data errors in the rail trip time distributions can have a strong effect on some reliability measures and because of the basic uncertainty about a proper measure of reliability, three measures of reliability can be suggested for the rail freight data:

1. Trip time standard deviation including moves over fifteen days
2. Trip time standard deviations excluding moves over fifteen days
3. Three-day percentage (of cars arriving in the last three-day period) including moves over fifteen days[19]

A major area of continued research is the study of network operations including the impacts of various policies on network performance. The network models which have been developed in the past are yielding many useful results, and separate extensions of these analyses should be quite cost-effective, given the existence of such models. In terms of data requirements, the current evidence suggests that cars moving in low-priority blocks, which are *not* necessarily low-priority cars, encounter serious movement unreliability problems. What is actually required is a more comprehensive analysis of the effects of block movement priorities and the development of improved movement control strategies for handling traffic in such blocks. In order to examine this problem closely, then, specific network data should be specially collected and analyzed.

A Synopsis of Railroad Passenger Service

One of the major national transportation crises until late 1973 was the gradual demise of rail passenger service in the United States. This downward spiral began soon after the end of World War II and has been attributed in general to the ascendancy of other modes of intercity passenger transportation, particularly air and automobile, the operating constraints imposed on the railroads by inflexible Interstate Commerce Commission constraints, and mismanagement, even neglect, on the part of the railroad companies themselves. These major factors, along with several others, combined to make rail passenger service in the United States essentially less attractive relative to other modes of intercity passenger transportation. Most railroads accumulated massive passenger service deficits throughout the 1960s, and in 1970, when the Penn Central Railroad which provided approximately 40 percent of the rail passenger service petitioned for bankruptcy, national intercity rail passenger service in the United States was on the verge of complete collapse.

As a result of this crisis, a semipublic agency, the National Rail Passenger Corporation (NPRC or AMTRAK), was established and assumed the operation of intercity rail passenger service in May 1971.[h] The existence of this agency and the contract relationship between AMTRAK and the railroad companies is unique in the transportation industries, adding still another dimension to the provision of transportation service in the United States.

Although the Rail Passenger Service Act states that "insofar as practicable, the Corporation (NRPC) shall directly operate and control all aspects of its rail passenger service," the corporation does not, in fact, exercise much direct control over the railroads which run the AMTRAK trains. NRPC has taken over responsibility for travel agent transactions and reservations, it owns about 350 passenger train cars and 300 locomotives, it employs some 800 station and terminal personnel, and it has assumed certain onboard functions such as the work done by stewards, cooks, waiters, and sleeping car attendants, but this hardly constitutes direct control over the actual operation of rail passenger service in the United States.[20] Thus the relationship between the National Rail Passenger Corporation and the railroads is not hierarchical while, theoretically, the railroads are responsible to AMTRAK.

Since the Interstate Commerce Commission is the primary source for historical information on rail passenger service, the reporting mechanisms are determined to a large extent by the requirements of the ICC. Other than improved ridership counts, on-time performance information, and surveys of passenger complaints or attitudes toward riding the trains, AMTRAK does not collect any rail passenger service data that are not already collected by the ICC. The monthly "blue forms" (NRPC Forms 6-10), for example, which the railroads file directly with AMTRAK, are selected items from the uniform system of accounts prescribed by the ICC.

The existence of AMTRAK has not significantly increased or improved the data available or the operation of rail passenger service. One of the most important and long-standing issues concerning data for rail passenger transportation service measures is simply the allocation of passenger costs. Over the years, the ICC has developed elaborate formulae to determine the costs assignable to rail passenger service. In some cases, the allocation of costs is clear, but in most cases (such as in the operation of a station that provides both freight and passenger service) an accurate allocation of costs is hardly possible. As a result,

---

[h]Only the Southern Railway Company, the Chicago, Rock Island, and the Pacific, and the Denver and Rio Grande Western continue to operate non-AMTRAK passenger trains. The Georgia Central offers periodic mixed trains with passenger service and the Toronto Hamilton and Buffalo (jointly owned by the Penn Central and the Canadian Pacific) offer passenger service between Buffalo and Toronto.

the ICC allocation formulae are suspect. The problem on rail passenger data is compounded further because the current contract relationship between the railroads and AMTRAK does not provide an incentive for the railroads to minimize the cost of rail passenger operations. While the ICC may collect a vast amount of information on the annual Form A documents, only a minor portion of the data is relevant to the construction of actual performance measures. As noted earlier, AMTRAK has not significantly increased the amount of information reported by the railroads or improved on the quality of the information reported. Neither the ICC nor AMTRAK collects information vital to establishing a measure of the quality and efficiency of rail passenger service in the United States. An obvious example of such a data gap is the lack of information on the condition of roadbeds, track, and rights-of-way. As AMTRAK slowly assumes more and more direct responsibility for the operation of rail passenger service in the United States, it will need to construct an information system that reflects the true indication of performance and cost.

**The Feasibility of Procuring Private
Source Data**

The glaring inefficiencies in rail operations appear to be those areas in which the available data are least organized. While railroads are not so different from other firms in being deluged with continual problems, the magnaminity of the railroad industry's most severe problems has been widely discussed. These problems include questionable practices in yard facilities, less-than-optimal train make-up operations, unloading procedures, branch-line utilization, and car allocation decisions, among others. If the issue of performance is to be taken seriously, than a mere comprehensive data file reflecting operations in these areas (as well as in the more traditional flow and stock accounts) must be developed. Furthermore, this data file should be organized to allow for continual updating and monitoring; it should be designed to provide regional and national aggregates; and it should be originated with the intention of being responsive to the needs of the empirical investigator over a long period of time.

As pointed out earlier, most of the currently published data must be sanctioned by the ICC or the Bureau of Census. The sheer volume of data which are available through these agencies is overwhelming; the usefulness is something else—the reams of paper with countless numbers than have been the target of anecdotes, jokes, and inquiries over several decades. Rarely has a classic example of the ratchet effect in the public arena been more apparent.

The need for a complete reevaluation and streamlining of the public data files is quite compelling for railroad input and output data and has been discussed elsewhere. Perhaps a more important need is to examine the possibilities of generating, collecting, and procuring data through private sources. While there are some obvious advantages and disadvantages to the use of private source information and its general availability, the limited applications of public source data for railroad operations suggested that serious attention be given to the private source path. The expectation is that some firms will shy away from providing data under the umbrella of propriety. With the current situation in the railroad industry, however, the issue of confidentiality becomes moot.

Comments on Measures of Industrial Performance

The size of the profit rate for a firm or industry should not be interpreted as a sole or an infallible indication of the effectiveness of competition. Rather, it is one of several dimensions of economic performance which must be regarded as a composite set of measures for evaluating the degree of competition. Normal and less-than-normal profits ordinarily are linked with certain models of competitive equilibrium whereas profits chronically in excess of some normal rate usually are associated with restrictions of outputs and undesirable income distribution effects. Public concern about the existence of the excess profit case in all modes of transportation during recent years need not be manifest. Profit rates and rates of return have been falling and in some cases approaching zero.

The prevalence of a low profit rate may be associated with adverse results on other levels (such as chronic excess capacity, rigid union work rules, and inflexible regulatory requirements), and any profit performance must be analyzed in the light of the rate of technical change, the trend of demand and various exogenous factors.

While the CAB and the Air Transport Association historically have been reluctant to pinpoint relative inefficiencies among air carriers, there is a widespread belief that a large part of the interfirm variations in economic performance may be attributed to differences in managerial abilities. This belief is reflected in the views of one carrier's president commenting on management prowess:

It is not really competition that has caused their (the firm's) problems. In fact, in many instances, it is the inability or failure of the large carriers to compete in efficiency that is the culprit—particularly in times when the national economy is sagging. It is their failure to forecast as accurately or react as rapidly as do some of their smaller competitors to changes in economic conditions.[21]

Several observers of historical airline industry performance have shared the opinion that carrier managements experience considerable variation in their abilities to control costs.[22] Furthermore, a carrier's cost performance can change sharply relative to that of the industry in a short period of time. Shifts in aircraft technology presumably have induced sharp reductions over the years in aircraft operating costs and consequently lowered the supply curve of air transportation. Almarin Phillips, in his study on the impacts of the aircraft industry, has argued that these shifts in technology have qualitatively affected the level of service for air passengers, induced fare reductions and thereby influenced the demand for air travel.[23]

Recent attention in market structure-performance studies has emphasized the importance of measuring profit risk.[24] The importance of verifying empirical relationships in the performance of oligopolistic and imperfectly competitive markets cannot be stressed too lightly. In fact, a coherent set of empirical relationships for these markets is presently available in the industrial organization literature.[25] Although the field of industrial organization has contributed much empirical evidence in recent years on the performance of various markets, its origin and its value rest more in efforts to encounter intricate problems of public policy than in testing market theories. Nevertheless, because of the large dispersion of equilibrium outcomes which are possible in imperfectly competitive market performance, and also in transportation firm performance, substantially more empirical work is appropriate in this area.

Notes

1. John M. Vernon, *Market Structure and Industrial Performance: A Review of Statistical Findings* (Boston: Allyn and Bacon, Inc., 1972), Ch. 2.

2. See especially F.M. Scherer, *Industrial Market Structure and Economic Performance* (Chicago: Rand McNally & Co., 1970), pp. 402-404; and Ann F. Friedlaender, *The Dilemma of Freight Transport Regulation* (Washington: The Brookings Institution, 1969), Ch. 4.

3. See T.M. Whitin, "Output Dimensions and Their Implications for Cost and Price Analyses," *Journal of Business* 45 (April 1972), pp. 305-315.

4. See Jack Hirshleifer, "The Firm's Cost Function: A Successful Reconstruction," *Journal of Business* 35 (July 1962), p. 241 n.

5. See George W. Wilson, "On the Output Unit in Transportation," *Land Economics* 35 (August 1959), pp. 266-76; also his *Essays on Some Unsettled Questions on the Economics of Transportation* (Bloomington, Ind.: Foundation for Economic and Business Studies, Indiana University, 1962).

6. See Charles E. Olson and Terence A. Brown, "The Output Unit in Transportation Revisited." *Land Economics* 48 (August 1972), pp. 380-82.

7. For example, most railroad rates for TOFC shipments are flat pre-trailer-trip rates. See Merrill J. Roberts and Associates, *Intermodal Freight Transportation Coordination: Problems and Potential* (Pittsburgh, Pa.: University of Pittsburgh, 1966), pp. 184-85.

8. Olson and Brown, "Output Unit," p. 281.

9. Consad Research Corporation, *Next Steps in Developing Suitable Output*

Measures for Transportation Systems, prepared for U.S. Department of Commerce, Pittsburgh (October 15, 1966) p.1.3.

10. Cambridge, Mass.: Harvard University Press, 1960.

11. See A.L. Morton, "Intermodal Competition for the Intercity Transport of Manufacturers," *Land Economics* 47 (November 1972), pp. 357-66.

12. U.S. Bureau of the Census, *1967 Census of Transportation*, Commodity Transportation Survey, Washington, D.C. 1971.

13. Morton, "Intermodal Competition."

14. See F.T. Bolger and H.W. Bruck, "An Overview of Urban Goods Movement Projects and Data Sources," U.S. Department of Transportation. Washington, D.C., June 1973, pp. 95-96 and 100-102.

15. U.S. Bureau of Census, *1967 Census of Manufactures, Industry Statistics*, vols. 1, 2, and 3, 1971.

16. Interstate Commerce Commission, Bureau of Economics, "Freight Revenue and Wholesale Value at Destination of Commodities Transportation by Class I line Haul Railroads in 1959," Washington, D.C., 1961.

17. Rate bureaus are simply not a source. One might use the *Carload Waybill Statistics 1969*.

18. For a strong verification of this point, see Northeast Corridor Transportation Project Final Report, vol. III, p. 26.

19. For the basis of the above discussion, see B.C. Kullman, *A Model of Rail/Truck Competition in the Intercity Freight Market*, Ph.D. dissertation, Department of Civil Engineering, Massachusetts Institute of Technology, 1973.

20. These statistics appear in the *1972 Annual Report* of the National Railroad Passenger Corporation, Washington, D.C., February 1973.

21. Statement by Robert Six, President of Continental Airlines to U.S. Congress Senate, Committee on Commerce, hearings before the Subcommittee on Aviation, *Economic Condition of the Air Transportation Industry*, February 1971, p. 300.

22. A selected number of observers include Harold D. Koontz, "Economic and Managerial Factors Underlying the Subsidy Needs of Domestic Trunk Line Carriers," *Journal of Air Law and Commerce* 18 (Spring 1951), pp. 114-15; Richard E. Caves, *Air Transport and Its Regulators* (Cambridge, Mass.: Harvard University Press, 1962), pp. 259-64; and Robert J. Gordon, "Airline Costs and Managerial Efficiency," in *Transportation Economics* (New York: National Bureau of Economics Research, 1965), pp. 88-91.

23. Almarin Phillips, *Technology and Market Structure: A Study of the Aircraft Industry* (Lexington, Mass.: Lexington Books, D.C. Heath and Co., 1971).

24. Roger Sherman, *Oligopoly: An Empirical Approach* (Lexington, Mass.: Lexington Books, D.C. Heath and Company, 1972), Ch. 11.

25. See Leonard Weiss, "Quantitative Studies of Industrial Organization," in Michael D. Intriligator, ed., *Frontiers of Quantitative Economics* (Amsterdam: North Holland Publishing Co., 1971), Ch. 9.

4 The Research Function of the Regulatory Commission

The creation of the Interstate Commmerce Commission (ICC) in 1887 was a general reflection of the trend toward more reliance upon administrative agencies in dealing with major social problems and a specific response to the unfolding railroad problem at that time. The complex and varied nature of the existing problems necessitated the creation of an agency with maneuverability and versatility and whose functions would not too greatly defy the traditional separation of powers principle. With the implementation of the Interstate Commerce Act, the railroads and rate-setting associations were required to adjust the rate determination process and rate structures to comply with the establishment of the commission.

The Transportation Act of 1920 instructed the Interstate Commerce Commission to prepare and adopt a plan for the consolidation of the railway properties of the United States into a limited number of systems. Following the Transportation Act of 1920, the ICC was converted from an agency devoted to facilitating private collusion to an "outright public cartel,"[1] which was vested with the power of minimum rate regulation, given control of entry into, exit from, and capital formation in the industry, and granted a variety of means for endeavoring to equalize the rate of return between the financially strong and weak railroads.[a] The prohibition of pooling prescribed in the original act of 1887 was changed to allow for discretionary approvals of pooling arrangements.[2] The famous Ripley consolidation plans for equalizing disparities among the various railroads were a result of the 1920 act, but the stronger railroads were not interested in assisting the limping ones and had the right to refuse under the vague prescriptions of the statute.[b]

As discussed in Chapter 1, the ICC among its other responsibilities also regulates the motor carrier industry. The Civil Aeronautics Board (CAB) is another independent regulatory commission, created in 1938, to provide administrative and statutory surveillance in the airline industry. For a thorough discussion of the institutional features and the legal apparatus of these and the

---

[a]The ICC provided a return of 5.5 percent on a fair value of investment as a target for 1920 and 1921, after which the target was 6 percent. If a railroad's rate of return exceeded the maximum, it was required to retain half the excess in a contingency reserve and to deposit the other half in a fund administered by the ICC for loan purposes to the weaker railroads. This provision proved unworkable, mainly because of the depression, and in 1933 the Emergency Transportation Act ended any effort at a target rate of return for the industry.

[b]In fact, the Transportation Act of 1940 repealed the Ripley plan for consolidations and substituted other criteria.

other independent regulatory commissions (as well as their interactions and conflicts with the various administrative agencies of the U.S. Department of Transportation), Professor Phillips has provided a valuable reference.[3] Alternatively, this chapter emphasizes potentially fruitful areas of inquiry which research staffs of these commissions might undertake.

The Role of Economic Analysis in the Regulatory Commission

The railroad industry shares with other regulated industries certain unique problems arising from the conduct of the regulatory body itself.[c] Thus, while the transportation industries are carrying on their day-to-day activities, the regulatory commissions should be scrutinizing their own criteria at the same time. For example, what criteria does the Interstate Commerce Commission (ICC) utilize to adjudicate mergers in the railroad industry? What are the relationships between the merger decisions and the performance aspects of the railroad companies? Do delays in the procedures of merger testimony detract from, or reduce, any of the industry performance aspects? If so, is there a better approach for handling merger cases which the ICC could adopt? These questions can provide the impetus for systematic approaches to evaluating the impacts of mergers and other changes in market structure in the railroad industry. The focus would be on the behavior of the railroad companies in view of structural considerations, technical change, merger related effects, and other efficiency issues.

When the research staffs of the regulatory commissions, or of the railroads, undertake an estimation of the costs of the prolonged proceedings of a merger case, some events transpire quite readily, such as straightforward consolidation projects. No cost analysis, however, can act adequately as a gauge for possibly the most vital long-run cost to the industry: the loss of intelligent, young management talent who simply cannot afford to "mark time" while doubt and apprehension concerning the merger outcome increase. The areas of manpower that are the most susceptible to loss are, not surprisingly, the ones where transfer of skill comes most readily: for example, law, industrial engineering, data processing, and marketing. Unfortunately, these are the types of skills upon which the companies and the railroad industry must depend for future development.

Not all manpower losses occur prior to merger. Nor are they precisely related

---

[c]Most of the following discussion pertains to the Interstate Commerce Commission and its regulation of the railroad industry. There is no a priori reason why the tenor of the analysis could not be extended to the motor trucking or airline industries, especially since the emphasis in this section is not on the institutional features of each industry (or agency) but rather on the mechanism of the regulatory process and the kinds of analyses which should be an automatic source of inquiry for any serious research staff.

to delay and indecision factors because the postmerger record in some instances also is scattered with departures of talent, some of whom by recognizing the values of their skills did not react favorably to the cajoling assurances of railroad life. Their marginal returns were simply higher elsewhere. If a new method which simply expedites the merger process is developed, the marginal returns to management in terms of span of control and satisfaction would be increased.

Several inferences can be made from the empirical results of various merger studies in the literature to suggest the paths which the Interstate Commerce Commission may follow with respect to its merger policy. One possible avenue of choice for the ICC is to continue its past policy of adjudicating merger applications on a case-by-case approach. Another is to consider the railroad industry as a structural arrangement with different levels of decision-making activities. In this sense, merger impacts could be analyzed in terms of the changes in the overall resulting structure. This approach then introduces a dynamic aspect to the merger with the method asserted as especially relevant for analyzing these impacts being that of optimal control theory.[d] Although a thoroughgoing study of this method requires a carefully constructed and rigorously developed model, the approach to the dynamics of discretionary and decision-making behavior proposed here might prove useful to the ICC if such an analysis is refined.

A Proposed Approach for Evaluating Railroad Mergers

The conventional theory of the firm has been generally developed in terms of static equilibrium. In terms of the dynamics, most research efforts have been concerned with the growth of aggregate phenomena, such as national economies, rather than microeconomic problems. Theorems have been developed to estimate growth paths of an economic system, but there have been no assessments of the paths which small firms follow in becoming larger firms, as we have indicated previously. One way in which firms in the railroad industry (large or small) become larger is through one facet of this growth process—namely, mergers.

Firms in the railroad industry presumably are organized in such a way to maximize their managerial goals subject to a set of constraints, including those imposed by the ICC. If the overall structure of the industry is designed to include a series of hierarchical decisionmakers (from the ICC down to the diesel mechanic of a given railroad), the structure with respect to each railroad will

---

[d]The approach has been discussed by the author with Edward Margolin, the former director of the ICC's Bureau of Economics, and with members of his staff. The outcome of the discussions is that, while the approach is theoretically appealing and some data support could be generated, its usefulness and feasibility are many years away.

operate with some specific degree of efficiency. If two railroads desire to merge, the ICC wishes to know, first, how the performance of the merged structure compares with the premerged configuration for given rail services; and second, how the performance of the merged structure changes over time as the levels of service change. These two criteria would become the conditions by which a dynamic model must describe and evaluate merger-generated changes in the structure of the railroad industry.

Although the method of analyzing dynamic models, known as optimal control theory, has been widely used in electrical engineering and mathematical programming areas, only recently has it entered the areas of mathematical economics and economic theory. An underlying assumption in adapting this method is that many of the activities of railroads are not unlike phenomena found in electrical engineering. In other words, a merger which induces a change in the efficiency of a participating railroad to ship goods over a specified distance in a given time period conceptually is analogous to the condition where an increase of power in an electric motor will move a mass or object over a certain distance in a given time interval.

The approach requires the consideration of the Interstate Commerce Commission as an organization which maintains the responsibility for supervising and regulating the affairs of the railroad industry.[e] If the ICC intends to function as an effective agency, then it will be dealing with complex systems which would include: (1) dynamic-optimal service processes, such as the quality and frequency of rail service between various city-pairs; (2) decision-making elements (designated controllers), who would adjudicate issues in the areas of company mergers, rates, abandonments, diversification efforts, and complaints; and (3) transmission lines which link the controllers and processes in a form of a hierarchical structure. The higher level controllers (the commission members) send information to the subsystems which would be lower levels of the hierarchic structure. The lower-level controllers would be responsible for the less important issues of railroad operations, such as handling local rate and tariff changes, operating violations, maintenance deficiencies, and the like. Of course, the global result produced by these subsystems is weakened considerably by either nonoptimal organization or poor transmission. The problem of a synthesis of organizational structures which are optimal represents a certain theoretical and practical interest. In order that this problem be solved, it is therefore necessary to introduce a measure of the quality of organizational structures from which an optimum structure can be selected.

Assume that the ICC consists of controlled dynamic processes ($P_1, P_2, \ldots, P_n$), local level controllers ($C_1, C_2, \ldots, C_n$), the overall controller (C)—the commission, transmission lines (L_i for $i = 1, 2, \ldots, n$), which link C with the n

---

[e]The affairs of the other transport modes which the ICC regulates by statutory requirement under its jurisdiction are ignored for the moment.

local level controller, and transmission lines (L_j for $j = 1, 2, \ldots, m$), which link the local level controllers with the Class I railroad companies (R_1, R_2, $\ldots$, R_m).

The behavior of the controllers can be specified through the use of objective functionals which, together with the process and constraint equations, can be used for the derivation of optimal control algorithms. Since the organizational composition of the ICC is the principal interest in this approach, attention should be devoted to the computation of the performance characteristics of the optimum regulatory process which are essential for the evaluation of organizational quality. The term OPC (optimum performance characteristic) has been used to denote this quality index with relatively little attention given to the derivation of the algorithms. While the mathematics of this approach have been presented elsewhere,[4] it is apparent from commentaries on the research of the approach that, irrespective of the policy constraints from the ICC, the expected postmerger structural and performance tendencies of firms in the railroad industry warrants further investigation.

Merger Criteria of the Interstate Commerce Commission

The ICC published its *Complete Plan of Consolidation* in 1929 under which any consolidation had to conform to the configuration designed in the plan and be in the public interest.[5] None of the consolidated systems proposed under the plan ever was effected, and very few rail consolidations occurred during the period of the 1920 statute. However, the Transportation Act of 1940 repudiated the concept of a master plan for rail unifications and instead insisted that all proposals to purchase, lease, merge, consolidate, or otherwise acquire control of railway properties would be examined on their own merits in light of certain criteria as specified by Congress in Sec. 5(2)(c) of the Interstate Commerce Act of 1887. The 1940 act redefined the criteria as:

(1) the effect of the proposed transaction upon adequate transportation service of the public; (2) the effect upon the public interest of the inclusion, or failure to include, other railroads in the territory involved in the proposed transaction; (3) the total fixed charges resulting from the proposed transactions; and (4) the interest of the carrier employees affected.[6]

In addition to the statutory requirements, the ICC seems to have adopted a set of "ad hoc" criteria, as a result of its being left to adjudicate each case "on its own merits." These criteria appear at various times in merger cases presented to the ICC. The ad hoc criteria involve: (1) speed of delivery; (2) economy and frequency of service; and (3) the appropriate provision and most efficient use of general and specialized transport facilities.[f] The ad hoc set actually has evolved as an attempt to clarify the ambiguities of the term *public interest*, which is specified in the statutory criteria, and to maintain some degree of intramodal, competitive traffic flow. The ad hoc criteria represent factors which are important determinants influencing traffic on given routes and have a direct bearing on shippers' choice of routes. Since mergers bring about structural changes, the protection of public and private interests with respect to routes and traffic volume are evaluated frequently in terms of the ad hoc criteria.

In an actual merger case, the applicants resort to demonstrating the beneficial impacts of what has been described above as the ad hoc set. The ICC then attempts to evaluate this deluge of favorable data with evidence which protestors and intervenors present.[g] It is assumed that under the binds of testimony the

---

[f]*Speed of delivery* indicates siding-to-siding elapsed time, apart from frequency or dependability. It is a vital factor in the handling of certain types of traffic, for example: perishable foods; livestock; freight forwarder traffic, generally consisting of high-class and high-value merchandise; export shipments, which must meet specified ship sailings; auto parts traffic, which must move virtually on an assembly line schedule; magazines, which must meet scheduled "release" dates; and piggyback traffic. *Frequency of service* facilitates the use of rail transportation as a "pipeline" in the total distribution pattern of any industrial or commercial enterprise. Steel mills, automobile manufacturing and assembly plants, and other plants that operate continuously can do a more effective job of gearing their shipping and receiving pattern to rail movement when frequent rail service is available—a frequently alleged merger benefit. Another consideration in frequency of service, although directly related to intermodal competition, also affects intramodal competition: namely, the flexibility of motor carrier schedules versus the fixed cutoff times which railroads must observe in order to meet scheduled train departures. Greater frequency of rail service provides some offset to this intermodal service handicap, and to the extent one railroad system (which might result from a merger) can provide this greater frequency of service, it also will have an intramodal advantage. For many shippers and receivers, dependability is the "priceless ingredient" of a service product and is a prime consideration in their routing selections. Inventory is an important element of total distribution cost and has always been so, but in earlier years the maintenance of a substantial inventory was accepted as a necessary burden. If dependability is lacking, the only insurance against "out-of-stock problems" and loss of sales is the expensive alternative of heavier inventory, which itself is a risk in those product lines where models and styles change frequently. *Specialized equipment*: Aside from the innovation of dieselization in the railroad industry, probably the most useful advance has been the development and implementation during the past five to ten years of specialized freight car equipment, including both specialized cars for the handling of particular products and large-capacity cars. Over that period, there has been a steadily increasing amount of specialized equipment demanded by shippers. Such equipment generally has one or both of two special purposes—to better protect the lading from damage, and/or to facilitate loading or unloading, occasionally as an integral part of the plant operation. The ability of a railroad to provide such specialized equipment is often decisive in shipping routing selections on the traffic involved and sometimes may also influence the routing of other traffic which moves in regular equipment. Whether the large-size railroads (or alternatively, merged railroads) are better able to provide specialized equipment in order to take advantage of economies of scale is an empirical issue. Part of the problem is that interfirm rentals and leasing arrangements provide similar functions for railroads in the absence of merger.

[g]The deluge is overwhelming. A typical volume of testimony contains approximately 400 pages, figures, and charts of information. An average finance docket consists of 300 volumes. At an extreme, the Penn Central case contained 954 volumes plus hundreds of separate exhibits. With all respect for due process, diminishing returns from additional testimony surely must occur early in proceedings.

applicants will carry out their promised and planned operating changes. Only occasionally does the ICC subsequently "spot-check" a unified railroad for confirmation purposes. This is one area in which the regulatory agency needs to improve its efforts.

The Responsibilities of the Regulatory Commission

Regulation may be regarded as a measure designed to alleviate any gaps between private and public interests which might arise. Traditionally, the regulatory commissions have operated via a system of rules concerning items such as rates, depreciation methods, rates of return, and so on. Yet the problem remains that the rules really provide no inducements to superior performance on the part of the firms. Quite frequently the rules or methods do not tell how or with what instruments a company could induce superior dynamic performance, such as its managerial decisions involving increased risk-taking, cost-reduction, service in-novation, and developing new markets. A consequence of the inherent limita-tions of regulations per se necessitates operating more as a restraining influence than as a positive impetus to good performance. These restraining influences exercised by the regulatory agencies can be interpreted in relation to the cartel stabilization features of regulation.[7] In practice, the ICC has devoted the major part of its efforts toward regulating selective competitive rate-cutting;[8] but this fact is not surprising, since this should be the primary duty of a cartel-stabilizing agency. Still, it remains to pose the following questions: if not regulation, what additional factors tend to explain why the performance of railroads has been as good as—or no worse than—it has been? Principal influences which are offered as answers are: the profit incentive, managerial needs, long-run decreasing costs associated with continuously increasing demand, technological considerations, elasticity of demand, intermodal competition, and finally, the threat of govern-ment competition.

Lags in Regulatory Impacts

A railroad prohibited from raising its rates or ordered to lower them may react by reducing the quality of its service. In theory, the ICC can prevent a railroad from degrading the quality of its services, but this would induce serious practical difficulties. To illustrate, if the waiting period for shipment arrivals lengthens, or the number of available boxcars decreases, or breakage is greater, or cars are less clean, the shipper may gain virtually nothing from a rate reduction. Yet these changes in the level of service, unless gross, are difficult to detect, prove, or rectify.

The whole issue of whether incentives are provided for railroad management is hardly solved by the accident of regulatory lag. Rates are periodically, and not continuously, equated with costs. During the periods between regulatory determination of a rate reduction, the railroad has a profit incentive to become more efficient. However, this lag feature probably does not provide much incentive to the railroads, because, first, it is an inadvertent method of injecting a profit incentive, and second, it is not certain that the opportunity provided by regulatory lag to obtain supranormal profits is sufficient to avoid serious disincentive effects, although those effects might be even greater if there were no lag. If a railroad achieves a technical innovation which enables it to reduce its costs and increase its profits significantly, the ICC, if it is reasonably alert, will act accordingly as the railroad's rate of return begins to increase. The railroad will receive some profits in the interim, although the profits may be so much less than without regulation that the railroad's efforts in pursuing future innovations are dampened.[h] An effectively regulated railroad, then, may be denied the minimum reward for inventive activity which a competitive firm would obtain. This analysis can be applied to the case when the inventive activity is merger. The inference is that mergers may not be undertaken as effectively with regulation.

If the railroads are effectively regulated, then an empirical investigation into their merger properties could shed some light on the above issues. It is in this context that more rigorous econometric analyses are proposed as appropriate investigations for the Interstate Commerce Commission. It is also a simple matter to extend this plea to the CAB for airline merger cases.

The Development of Performance Measures
for Railroad Freight Operations

Productivity and performance are the key variables on which a regulatory agency should have knowledge in order to assess the impacts of a change in market structure. The general problems associated with productivity measurement, interpretation, and explanation are the subject of an extensive literature. The wide-ranging works of W.E.G. Salter[9] and J.W. Kendrick[10] provide a foundation for analyzing and developing improved productivity and performance measures.

The usual approach in the analysis of performance measures and productivity change is to focus on the very limited usefulness of the time-honored but *partial* (Kendrick's term) productivity ratio of output per unit of labor input (in terms of either man-years or man-hours). At a later stage of his 1961 analysis, Kendrick used the more general ratio of output per unit of total factor input, that is, per unit of combined labor and capital input. Either ratio can be useful

[h]Of course, the explanation of railroads' reluctance to pursue innovation may be benign. An attempt to quantify the relationship between different size railroads and their rate of innovation (technical progress) appears warranted.

in measuring the saving in inputs over time due to all causes, but it cannot measure total changes in productive efficiency. Such changes are affected by shifts in the composition of total factor input as factors are substituted for each other when relative factor prices and the techniques of production change over time.

These considerations lead naturally to the perception that the production function underlies all meaningful analysis of productivity change. Despite formidable difficulties which are simultaneously conceptual, theoretical, and practical and which stem from the presently incomplete state of both the theory of production and of the knowledge of input and output flows, it is considered essential to attempt to apply an interpretive treatment of productivity flows in railroad operations. This treatment would include the fitting of a set of production functions to existing data. An interpretive treatment of shifts in productive efficiency is not fully explanatory of such movements in the railroad industry. Rather, it is a first stage analytical process which provides estimates in quantitative terms of the distribution of the several sources of a given amount of movement of unproductive efficiency. Beneath these sources lie the fundamental causes which also can be subject to explanatory analyses and to empirical testing.

Inasmuch as any railroad system consists of a number of subsystems or parts which have some common objectives and functions operating effectively with varying degrees of independence, a system's efficiency as a service function can be measured in view of its technology and its cost, time, and responsiveness to natural and individual needs. The most important stylized fact underlying this technology is that technical change reflects the major source of industrial, and particularly railroad, economic growth.[11] The basic method employed in reaching this conclusion is to compare the rate of growth of output with a weighted average of growth of inputs. The difference, or residual, is customarily assumed to be the rate of technical change.

Performance measures in the historical sense (that is, using time series, cross-sectional, or pooled data) typically have provided a basis only for making crude comparisons among different sets of operators (industries or firms, generally). They do not in and of themselves reflect any measurement of causality, either in the sense of how a set of inputs affects output within the same industry (railroad) or in the sense of how operating practices of one railroad affect the performance of other contiguous railroads. They do, however, provide a critical foundation on which causality can be imputed through the linkage of a set of production and cost functions.

The crucial linkages among outputs, inputs, and their performance are illustrated in Figure 4-1, which is a flow chart depicting the theoretically correct way to estimate costs in railroad operations. Cost functions usually depict cost as a function of output, whereas performance measures merely are ratios of outputs to inputs. The production function, however, is necessary to specify the

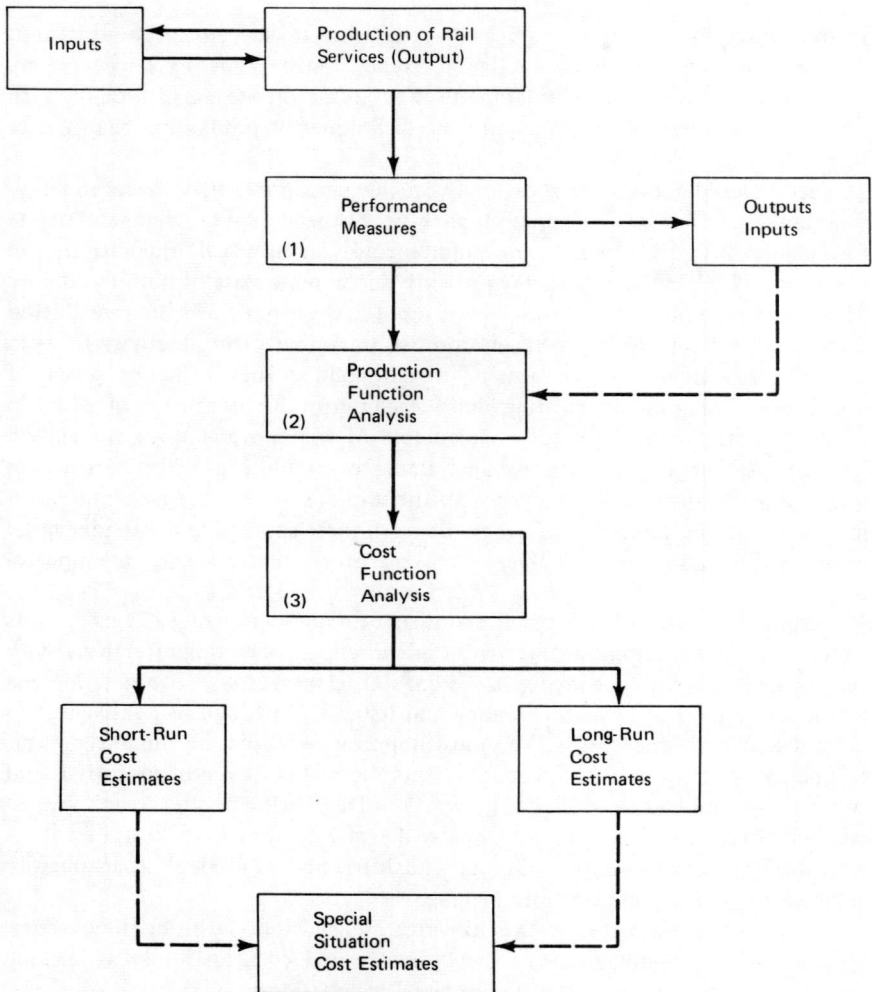

Figure 4-1. Flow Chart of the Derivation of Cost Functions in Railroad Operations

behavioral relationship between these outputs and inputs; it is the crucial functional relationship and is discussed in the next section.

A fairly broad coverage of literature has been devoted to various aspects of performance measures, particularly in the railroad industry. In order that any given performance measure be usable, several operating criteria must be specified:

1. The industry
2. The level of analysis
   a) Interfirm
   b) Intrafirm
3. Modal or intermodal
4. The time period
5. The level of aggregation
   a) Regional
   b) Divisional
   c) Corridor
   d) Link-specific (O-D pair)
      (1) Summation of selected links
      (2) Network specific

Once these specifications are made, a performance measure is constructed by selecting a relevant output and input and combining them (usually as a ratio of output to input) into a single measure. In theory, this step can be conducted on all possible combinations, but in practice only the set of "feasible" combinations should be considered. Assuming that these calculations are undertaken on cross-sectional data only, the performance measures can be displayed as a matrix of ratios between output and inputs, as is suggested by Table 4-1, which is segmented into nine different (although occasionally overlapping) categories:

1. Financial measures
2. Disaggregate cost measures
3. Operational measures
4. Labor force measures
5. Inventory measures
6. Reliability measures
7. Energy measures
8. Environmental measures
9. Accessibility measures

These items are discussed in detail elsewhere but are presented here merely to be suggestive of the direction in which an analysis of improved performance measures could lead.[i]

These major measures represent the following dimensions of activities: finance, disaggregate expense, operations, inventory, work force, reliability, energy, environment, and accessibility. Each category or measure can be subdivided into more detailed components and then into its basic elements. The following discussion highlights these major measures and some selected compo-

---

[i]A comprehensive analysis of multimodal measures is in progress under U.S. Department of Transportation sponsorship to MIT's Urban Systems Laboratory.

nents and elements of major importance to the specification and understanding of the flow chart which appears in Figure 4-1.

Financial Measures. These measures represent the managerial and monetary performances of agencies providing transportation services. The measures reflect the traditional balance sheet and income statement entries as prescribed by standard business-firm accounting practices. Financial measures suggest a specific dimension of performance (and ultimately of service) by focusing on the basic incentive of all business enterprises: profit.

The measures can be divided into two components: operational and consolidated. Operational financial measures pertain to only those areas of the agency which relate to strictly transportation operations, like operating revenues and operating expenses. Consolidated financial measures are more comprehensive since they cover all phases of the agency, including noncarrier investments. Items like rate of return and cash flow are extremely important measures of performance, but their uses must be treated with caution. For example, rates of return can be sharply different depending on their respective denominators.

In the operational financial measures, two widely used entries are working capital and the operating ratio. Working capital is a standard term, representing the difference between current assets and current liabilities, and is comparable across modes. Operating ratio, however, is more mode specific. It is the ratio of operating expenses to operating revenues and is reported as such in the trucking industry; it also can be calculated easily for the other modes.

Disaggregate Cost Measures. In a certain sense, these measures are subsets of the expense measures discussed above (operational or consolidated). Yet these measures appear sufficiently important to justify a separate analysis. Annual investment expenditures reflect an extremely valuable measure by itself. The other measures are disaggregated into the four principal levels of transportation activities: terminal, yard, road (or line-haul), and system. The purpose of this categorization is to focus on particular sectors of the transportation system as a method of isolating problems and as a basis for deriving statistical constructs, as will be discussed in the next section.

Operational Measures. These measures depict the strict operations of the transportation system. For example, in Table 4-1, total revenue ton miles (the second line item under "Operational Measures") could be calculated for any mode and could be split between common and contract carrier movements. In the case of passenger volumes, total revenue passenger miles would be the sum of the number of X revenue passengers transported Y miles by rail, bus or air modes (and auto, if it were included). In general, these measures refer to the physical activities of the transportation system and are to be distinguished from purely financial and economic (cost) measures.

Table 4-1
Selected Transportation Performance Measures

Financial Measures: Operational

Total operating revenue
Total operating expenses
Total operating income
Net operating income
Working capital
Operating ratio

Financial Measures: Consolidated

Total revenue
Total expenses
Total income
Net income
Rate of return on investment
Rate of return on stockholders'
  equity
Cash flow

Disaggregate Cost Measures

Investment in fixed plant and
  equipment
Terminal expense by category
Yard expense by category
Line haul expense by category
System expense by category

Operational Measures

Total revenue tons (passengers)
Total revenue ton-miles (passenger-
  miles)
Unit miles
Unit hours
Average length of haul
Average speed per unit
Unit loadings
  (loading and unloading efficiency)

Labor Force Measures

Number of employees by type
Man-hours worked
Man-hours paid for

Inventory Measures

Number of power units
Vintage of power units
Number of transport units
Vintage of transport units
Number of terminals/yards
Vintage of terminals/yards
Number of new units purchased
Number of refurbished units
Number of inoperative units
Percentage of equipment leased

Reliability Measures

Variance of unit arrivals
Variance of unit departures
Variance of running time
Number of misconnections
Delay minutes
Frequency of delay
Loss and damage payments

Energy Measures

Total amount of fuel consumed
Total cost of fuel consumed
Total BTU's consumed

Environmental Measures

Pollutant emissions per unit mile
Noise levels per unit

Accessibility Measures

Number of SMSA's served
Percent of SMSA's served
Total population of SMSA's served
Capacity of parking facilities
  available
Public transportation available

Labor Force Measures. These measures indicate the number and types of employees available to transportation firms and agencies. A general division can be made between management and union workers or between operating and nonoperating employees. An important distinction is between man-hours worked and man-hours paid for; the former is useful as an input to the amount of time actually worked (as an input to productivity), whereas man-hours paid for includes fringe benefits, work-rule practices and other nonwork time which contractually represents an expense to the firm. With the exception of rail data collected by the ICC, data for these two man-hour measures do not appear to be available yet for the other modes.

Inventory Measures. These measures are related to the stock of capital which transportation companies or agencies own or lease in order to offer their transportation services to shippers and to the public. The measures simply pertain to the quantity of units and to their average age or vintage. Their purpose is to focus on the amount of power available and the degree of obsolescence of the equipment—a logical source of productivity and quality of service.

Reliability Measures. Reliability might be the most significant variable affecting shippers' choice (and possibly passengers' choice in commuter and urban travel) as suggested by several shipper surveys. Unfortunately, very little data are available on the variable, except from company sources. A more detailed discussion of this measure is presented below.

Energy and Environmental Measures. These measures are published for all common carrier modes and represent the amount of energy consumed, its cost, and its by-products. A need for data relating these measures to the automobile mode is a task of the Department of Transportation or the Federal Energy Office.

Accessibility Measures. A necessary requirement for future empirical information on improved service measures is the acquisition of accessibility measures. A thorough investigation of SMSA, SEA, county, and regional frameworks is required in order to assess the best estimates of accessibility measures. Most of these data are readily available. Any presently unavailable or newly required data might be generated through existing institutions like the Federal Reserve District Banks, real estate development associations, railroad terminal companies, private nonprofit research groups, and industrial development agencies of state governments.

The Estimation of Production Functions
for Railroad Freight Operations

The estimation of production functions is becoming a frequently used procedure for identifying the growth component attributable to progress in all industries, including transportation. A production function describes the maximum quantity of output obtainable from any quantitative combination of the physical inputs that are included in the function. If Q represents output, L stands for labor input, and K for capital input, then a production function may be written as $Q = f(L, K)$. Quite obviously, this measure requires estimates of both inputs and outputs and of the behavioral linkage between the two in the form of the coefficients of the production function.

There are at least three principal reasons for suggesting a production function approach to the development of improved productivity measures. The first is the general desirability for accuracy, precision, and clarity to facilitate scientific analysis. A second and related reason concerns a particular objective: if it is known a priori why performance in railroad operations should be measured, then it is easy to decide what kinds of measures of inputs and outputs are appropriate. Statistical testing then becomes the means by which this appropriateness is determined.

A third reason for being concerned with the production function approach relates to the infrastructure of general cost analysis and to the estimation of cost functions.[12] The statistical estimation of cost functions has been in the strict sense an empirically evasive effort despite the literature being replete with different sorts of estimation attempts.[13] The chief reason for a paucity of meaningful estimates is that rarely are the cost functions related to the behavioral properties of the production functions from which costs should be derived. In past studies researchers, in their haste to relate costs to output, ignored the theoretical and practical linkages between production functions and output and between production functions and costs.

Conventional microeconomic theory describes the importance and requirements of specifying production functions prior to the estimation of costs. Expressed simply, it is essential that the appropriate form of a production function for each railroad (that is, the behavioral and statistical relationship between output and input) be specified before any meaningful costs can be estimated. In other words, accurate cost functions can be derived only when each underlying production function is specified and when certain assumptions (such as cost minimization) are maintained (again, refer to Figure 4-1).

As an example, one research study has investigated the specification and empirical testing of six alternative forms of production functions for railroad operations at the interfirm level of analysis in which published ICC and AAR data were being used.[14] The deterministic versions (that is, excluding error terms) of these production functions are the following:

1. Linear $\qquad Z = A + a_1 K + a_2 L + a_3 E$

2. Log-Linear $\qquad Z = A K^{a_1} L^{a_2} E^{a_3}$

3. Cobb-Douglas $\qquad Z = A K^{a_1} L^{a_2} E^{a_3}$ where $a_1 + a_2 + a_3 = 1$

4. Constant Elasticity of Substitution $\qquad Z = A [\delta K^{-\rho} + (1 - \delta) L^{-\rho}]^{-\upsilon/\rho}$

5. Embodied Technical Change $\qquad Z = A (e^{\lambda} K^{a_1}) L^{a_2} E^{a_3}$

6. Disembodied Technical Change $\qquad Z = A e^{\lambda} (K^{a_1} L^{a_2} E^{a_3})$

where
Z = output measure
A = intercept term (efficiency measure)
K = capital input
L = labor input
E = energy input
a_1, a_2, a_3 = elasticities of output with respect to the respective inputs

λ = rate of technological change
δ = distribution parameter
ρ = substitution parameter
υ = homogeneity parameter

The analysis was conducted on particular input/output measures for Class I railroads in the Southern Region (Southern District) as published by the Interstate Commerce Commission in *Transport Statistics in the United States: Part I, Railroads* for the years 1962 through 1972. Separate statistical procedures were employed for road-haul and yard operations on the assumption that production and cost functions underlying these respective activities manifest differing characteristics. As a starting point, ton-miles-revenue freight-road service was selected as the measure of output. Inputs for the road and yard analyses were chosen on the basis of two criteria—the availability of data that could be differentiated between these respective functions and a capability to allocate the data among capital, labor, and energy.

The purpose of this reference is to indicate one important use for the development of improved performance measures. Other uses can be suggested by referring back to Figure 4-1, which depicts the crucial role of service measures in the chain of causality between the basic inputs and outputs of any mode and the more elaborate economic analyses pertaining to production and costs. This figure traces the incorporation of the basic data into performance measures, then to constructs, then to the behavioral specifications of production functions, and finally to a range of cost-function estimations. Tracing the flow backward would lead to the following conclusion: In order to accurately estimate costs (for any transportation activity), logically one must specify the appropriate production function, which in turn requires an appropriate set of performance measures. And herein lies the intrinsic value of the flow chart in Figure 4-1.

The Estimation of Cost Functions for
Railroad Freight Operations

The dominant characteristic of a railroad's operations is its multiple-service function. Included in these multiple services are freight and passenger service, yard and line-haul service, bulk and less-than-carload commodities, perishable and merchandise traffic, and terminal services. In many studies of railroad costing, the extent of joint operations and fixed cost has involved a heavy reliance on statistical estimates of railroad cost.

One of the primary difficulties in specifying a production function for railroad operations is to differentiate the purely individual from the joint effects. Once the appropriate level of specification is determined in the production function, then plausible and accurate estimates of cost can be made.

Numerous costing methods have been used at various times and for varyious purposes by transportation analysts. In fact, in very few other industries have different techniques of costing been experimented and pioneered. This is largely due to the inherent difficulties of costing the joint service operations that so abound in the transportation industries.

The traditional method for estimating a long-run cost function is to fit the following relationship over a cross-section of firms:

$$TC = a + bZ \tag{4.1}$$

where TC is a vector of total cost observations, Z is a vector of output observations (such equations sometimes contain more than one output variable), and a and b are the intercept and slope respectively; they usually are assumed to be linear, but sometimes they are log-linear or have a squared output term. For this procedure to yield a long-run cost function, it is necessary to assume that each firm in the sample adjusts all its inputs so as to minimize costs. In the case of the railroad industry, there is reason to doubt that this is being done, simply because of the indivisibility of the railroad plant and because of the slowness of the regulatory agencies to grant approval to proposed track abandonments.[j] As a result, the railroad plant is in many cases likely to be overbuilt.

---

[j]One of the problems in using data collected from the proceedings of abandonment proceedings is that the railroad companies tend to overestimate the costs of the services which they are proposing to abandon.

Production function analysis in the railroad industry is complicated not only by the fixity and indivisibility of the physical plant but also by the variety of services provided using that plant. A study of railroad costs must recognize this multiple-product (service) nature of the railroad firm.[15] One way to handle the complication is to specify two separate types of output: gross ton-miles of freight service and gross car-miles of passenger service. More output variables are desirable and can be incorporated, but some simplification is necessary to make estimation feasible as a first attempt. In general, it can be argued that passenger and freight service are provided according to separate production functions, but they have one very important element in common: both use the same physical plant, which is fixed. If the amount of physical plant available to a railroad firm can be measured in terms of track mileage, then two separate production functions can be specified relating each type of output to inputs unique to it and the track services allocated to it. With fixed trackage, this yields a joint short-run cost function for both types of output.

To derive such a short-run cost function, assume a modified Cobb-Douglas production function, with no restriction on returns to scale. The production functions for freight and passenger service can then be written, respectively, in the following deterministic forms:

$$Z_f = AT_f^{a_1} R_f^{a_2} F_f^{a_3} L_f^{a_4} \tag{4.2}$$

and

$$Z_p = BT_p^{b_1} R_p^{b_2} F_p^{b_3} L_p^{b_4} \tag{4.3}$$

where Z_f and Z_p represent gross ton-miles of freight and passenger service, respectively, L represents labor input, F represents fuel input, R represents rolling stock input, T represents plant input (track and related structures), and the subscripts f and p refer to factor inputs allocated to freight and passenger service, respectively.[16] The short-run problem for a railroad firm is to adjust fuel, rolling stock, and labor to each service in order to minimize costs for any output level and to allocate the services of the fixed factor, trackage, between the two outputs to minimize costs. Since the railroads are regulated common carriers, they must carry all traffic at existing regulated rates; hence it is feasible that they treat output as exogenous and attempt to minimize costs. Mathematically, the problem is as follows: minimize

$$TC = r_1 (T_f + T_p) + r_2 (R_f + R_p) + r_3 (F_f + F_p) + r_4 (L_f + L_p) \tag{4.4}$$

subject to (4.2) and (4.3) as constraints, plus the additional constraint that

$$T = T_f + T_p \tag{4.5}$$

where the r's represent rentals on the various factors and T is the fixed amount of trackage for a given railroad.

The solution to this minimization problem can be derived through one grand lagrangean expression. While the mathematics are presented elsewhere,[17] suffice it to say that the procedure involves the separate derivations of short-run cost functions for freight and passenger service assuming given allocations of trackage and then a derivation of a joint short-run cost functions from the two separations. The long-run cost functions then can be derived from the short-run cost functions by differentiating short-run costs with respect to both outputs, applying first order conditions, and solving for Z_f and/or Z_p.

The Relationship between Short-Run and Long-Run Cost Functions

The most popular form of production function model has been the Cobb-Douglas function, which is a special case of the CES form.[k] Using isoquant analysis, the relation between the long-run and short-run cost functions can be shown graphically.[18] In order to derive these functions for the Cobb-Douglas production function form, one can consider a single-product, two-input competitive model, as depicted in Figure 4-2, which illustrates the derivation of the expansion path OP for this model. The expansion path in Figure 4-2 is nonlinear to indicate the general case; yet, if the production function is homogeneous, the expansion path must be a straight line.

The path OP is a long-run expansion path. In considering the analogous function in the short-run, that is, a "short-run expansion path," the quantity of factor K (capital) is held to be fixed at $\overline{K}$ and the horizontal line $\overline{K}S$ then defines the short-run expansion path. To increase output in the shortrun, the firm can only increase the quantity of L (labor) since K is fixed at $\overline{K}$.

Long-run and short-run cost functions may be derived by an examination of the long-run and short-run expansion paths. The long-run expansion path OP in Figure 4-2 provides the information for the long-run cost function as does the short-run path $\overline{K}S$ for the short-run cost function. For example, one point on OP is the tangency between isoquant Z_2 and isocost line C_2 which is plotted in Figure 4-3 when total cost is measured vertically and total output horizontally. Plotting all other points on the long-run expansion path OP results in the long-run cost function $LRTC$.

The same procedure may be performed for the short-run function. That is,

---

[k]Since its introduction in 1928, no single form has been more widely used. The reasons for this are several: it is simple to explain; it is a plausible form in that it displays constant returns to scale (which happens also to be the dominant empirical observation in transportation) and diminishing returns to an input; it is relatively easy to handle in connection with questions of aggregation; and it is easily estimated by standard regression techniques.

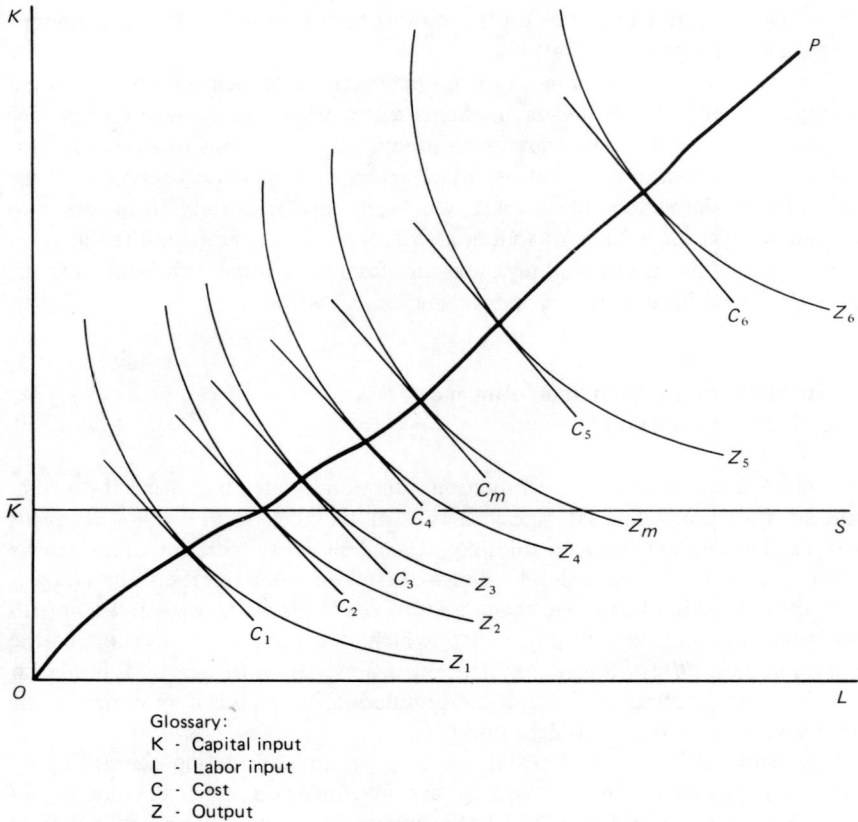

Figure 4-2. The Derivation of Expansion Path OP

transfer the cost-output values defined by each point on $\overline{KS}$ in Figure 4-2 to Figure 4-3. The result is the short-run cost function *SRTC*. In Figure 4-2, the two expansion paths have one point in common; that is, the intersection point which corresponds to an output of Z and a cost of C_2. In Figure 4-3, this same point is the tangency point between *SRTC* and *LRTC*. At all other output levels, *SRTC* exceeds *LRTC* since in the long run all inputs are variable with each level of output produced at minimum possible cost. In short run, however, the firm does not have perfect flexibility and is constrained by the invariability of input K.

Several properties of Figure 4-3 are interesting. The short run cost function has a positive intercept on the C axis, while the long-run function begins at zero. This reflects the fact that fixed costs exist only in the short run. Also, *SRTC* becomes vertical at an output level of Zm, while *LRTC* begins to increase. The

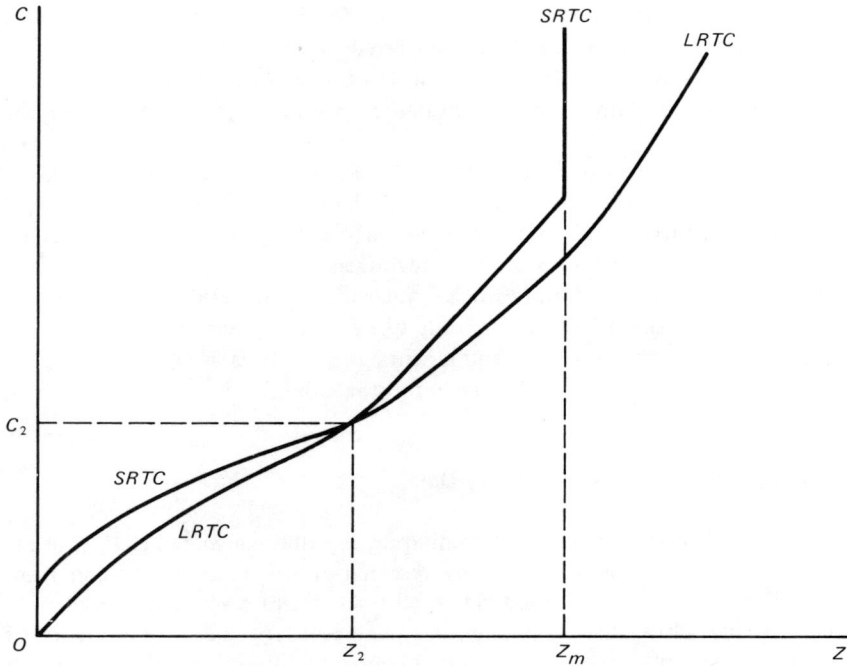

Glossary:
C - Cost
Z - Output
m - Capacity (short run)
SRTC - Short-run total cost
LRTC - Long-run total cost

Figure 4-3. Cost Equilibrium

explanations for these two phenomena are quite different. The *SRTC* function rises because of the law of diminishing returns, that is, with the application of more and more L to the fixed quantity of the other factor $\overline{K}$. The *LRTC* function rises because of the assumption that decreasing returns to scale occur at relatively high output levels.

Special Equipment Situations and Estimation of Long-Run Marginal Costs

From the long-run cost function, one can calculate "average" costs (or "marginal") of special car movements. These estimates are designed to reflect the cost of special order situations, like the cost of dispatching a switcher engine to deliver one auto parts car to a "preferred" customer, or like the cost of running "scheduled" extra trains. Extreme caution must be exercised, however, in developing these estimates since each figure is valid only under certain specific assumptions.

As an example, consider two types of equipment operating on a given railroad: a grade A boxcar for general merchandise and an unnamed special equipment car. First, long-run marginal cost will vary by length of haul. Second, the various cost estimates must be categorized. Finally, service differentials between rail and trucking need to be quantified. The results should suggest sharply reduced marginal costs for both types of equipment as length of haul increases.[19] For any piece of equipment, this analysis is appropriate. The problem remains one of generating the appropriate data.

The Availability of Internal Company Data

The traditional models of railroad production describe aggregate behavior in the industry. Newer models developed by research groups in some railroad firms were designed to predict how individual railroads might react to the problem of choice among alternative combinations of inputs for given movements of tonnage. In particular, the use of internal company data can provide important insight into the performance features of line-haul and yard movements. But usually, data can be assembled only in rather aggregated form, reflecting composite input choices for different commodities and hauls over many sections of each railroad (or division of a railroad). Not only are current data unable to be broken down into items depicting individual situations but, more importantly, certain cost figures in the formulation cannot be assembled at all.[1] Confronted with insuperable problems of collecting certain requisite data, it is necessary to use system averages in some cases and occasionally "ballpark" estimates in others for estimating certain types of costs. Still, the linkages in the theory must be acknowledged.

Subsequent procedures should be developed to provide railroad managements and agencies with a means for periodic updating of the numerical factors and cost coefficients through utilization of available economic data. In view of the need for more disaggregate information pertaining to internal company operations, it is recommended that railroad companies make available and accessible to researchers internal data on operations. To the extent that at least one research effort has opened some doors through the generous assistance of the Southern Railway System, it is hoped that subsequent work along these lines

---

[1]The indication of this difficulty should not detract from the overall merits of using data which are more disaggregate than those published in ICC records. To the extent that some internal data prove useful, this effort then should be regarded as quite rewarding.

will prove successful.[m] Rarely does the opportunity exist to use internal company data in order to test economic hypotheses. Such an opportunity in which selected data were provided by operating departments of the Southern Railway System in both Atlanta and Washington. While the methodology was exploratory and the results of the statistical analyses were tentative, on balance the findings do confirm some of the basic tenets of neoclassical production and cost theory—a body of knowledge heretofore untested at the intrafirm level.

Like the adage in computer circles of "garbage in, garbage out," the results of any cost estimate can only be as effective as its inputs. To say that the cost of a movement of boxcars is so many dollars can be accurate only if certain conditions are met. The cost estimate will be purely spurious unless the following elements are specified: the railroad itself, type of equipment, type of movement, location of movement, weather conditions, time of day, day of month, and other institutional considerations.

Future research efforts at the company level could extend the range of empirical inquiries in the railroad industry into other areas. Some of these research areas are long overdue and, as yet, essentially unexplored. These would include whole areas of research on the demand aspects, on behavioral and managerial issues, on regulatory impacts, and on the financial operations of firms in the railroad industry. These areas are of particular interest both to the rail companies themselves, especially in the context of understanding one another's behavior at the disaggregate level, to researchers who can expand their repertoire of empirical verification of important microeconomic principles, and especially to the regulatory commission members who can pursue their roles of surveillance with renewed confidence.

Summary

Statistical cost estimates of transportation operations must be interpreted and used with caution. Limitations on publicly available data restrict empirical cost estimates to applications only for generalized situations. While it is extremely difficult to obtain cost estimates for specific operations, it is important to obtain average or typical cost figures which may be used for the broad purpose of managerial regulatory policies.

The cost coefficients in some statistical studies in the railroad industry represent estimates of railroad cost characteristics for operations conducted under average operating conditions and may directly affect regulatory problems and costing. The influence of variables excluded from any analysis will be

[m]The work was part of a coordinated research effort under sponsorship by the Federal Railroad Administration, U.S. Department of Transportation to MIT with assistance from the Southern Railway System. A series of additional reports on the results of this coordinated research are forthcoming in 1974 and will be available from FRA offices in Washington, D.C.

consequential if the factors have a systematic effect on the costs. Even should such systematic, nonrandom factors modify the results, the influence may be accommodated by making slight procedural adaptations or by including additional information about the cost structure in order to transform averages into estimates better suited to special situations. Rough adjustments for the systematic influence of omitted variables can be made by obscuring any consistent tendency in the statistical errors of estimate. Also, if something is known about the approximate ordinal magnitude of cost differences for separate output or fixed capital input categories that have been aggregated into one variable in the cost analysis, then deviations from the norms can be accounted for by recomputing outputs or capital inputs. Observed results simply may be better than any available alternative.

From all of this emerges a really basic question: What is the relationship between market structure and market performance? The degree of such a relationship has been an often-debated and well-documented topic, with proponents ranging from one extreme to the other. Suffice it to say that, if the testimony of many participants in transportation merger cases is an indicator, it appears that (at least in the transportation industries) changes in market structure induce changes in market performance. If the regulatory commissions in the future regard their adjudicating roles in merger cases seriously, then substantial research must be undertaken linking the forecasts of expected changes in economic performance to changes in market structure resulting from merger activities (where a merger is only one form of a change in market structure).

The independent regulatory commissions must function and perform their responsibilities within the severe constraint of very limited funds. Questions of effectiveness, therefore, would center on the ways in which these funds are allocated by each commission to its respective tasks. With this background in mind, the above chapter has examined some possible paths for fruitful research on theoretically and practically appealing issues in the transportation industries. While the discussions have emphasized the freight sector of the railroad industry and the Interstate Commerce Commission, the implications can be extended easily to other transportation industries and their respective commissions. The essential point of this chapter is that there are selected lessons to be learned from previous research in the industrial organization and applied microeconomic fields. Foremost among the beneficiaries of these lessons should be the research staffs of the regulatory commissions. Otherwise, the "due process of law" considerations, evidenced in every litigation case or question of policy before the commissions, will continue to be an expensive charade.[20]

Notes

1. Many writers have espoused the view but none has pursued it more vigorously than Professor Hilton. See George W. Hilton, "What Went Wrong," *Trains* 27 (January 1967), p. 42.

2. For an inquiry into the effects of cartel agreements on rates, tonnage shares, and profits of the major eastern railroads in the last three decades of the nineteenth century, see Paul W. MacAvoy, *The Economic Effects of Regulation: The Trunk-Line Railroad Cartels and the Interstate Commerce Commission before 1900* (Cambridge, Mass.: MIT Press, 1965). According to MacAvoy (p. 14) there were four major reorganizations of the cartel, each of which was occasioned by failures from "cheating" by some of the members. Each reorganization was an attempt to provide means for detecting deviations from the agreed rates and to provide penalties for such deviations. In general, if it was possible for an individual railroad to increase its profits by being loyal to a cartel agreement rather than being disloyal, the cartel would likely be stable. However, the evasion of regulation by individual railroads and the reduction of the powers of the ICC by the courts induced the eventual collapse of cartel rates.

3. See Charles F. Phillips, Jr., *The Economics of Regulation: Theory and Practice in the Transportation on Public Utility Industries*, rev. ed. (Homewood, Ill.: Richard Irwin, Inc., 1969).

4. See J. Kneafsey, "The Treatment of Mergers in the Railroad Industry: An Optimal Control Theory Approach," Paper presented at the Annual Meeting of the *Operations Research Society of America*, New Orleans, April 1972.

5. *In the matter of Consolidation of the Railways of the United States into a Limited Number of Systems*, 159 ICC 522 (1929).

6. *The Transportation Act of 1940*, Sec. 5(2).

7. As mentioned earlier in this chapter, cartels were elaborate organizations set up by agreements among the railroads for setting rates (principally on grains) in the 1870s and 1880s. A discussion of cartel theory, in terms of an analysis of the ways in which cartels tend to increase the profits of their members and an analysis of the conditions in which they tend to be unstable, is beyond the scope of this paper. One of the best discussions is referenced in note 2 (above): MacAvoy, *Economic Effects of Regulation*, esp. pp. 13-24, where he states the conditions and requirements that a cartel arrangement must meet in order to operate successfully.

8. In a given year, say 1962, the Suspension Board of the ICC considered 5,170 tariffs out of a total of more than 173,000 filed in that year. Of the ones considered, about 95 percent involved rate decreases. See Merton J. Peck, "Competitive Policy for Transportation?" in Almarin Phillips, ed., *Perspectives on Anti-Trust Policy*, p. 257.

9. Salter, W.E.G., *Productivity and Technical Change* (Cambridge, England: Cambridge University Press, 1960).

10. Kendrick, John W., *Productivity Trends in the United States* (Princeton: Princeton University Press, 1961).

11. Early works suggesting this result in the aggregate include: Moses Abramovitz, "Resource and Output Trends in the United States Since 1870," *American Economic Review Papers and Proceedings* 46 (May 1965), pp. 5-23; Robert M. Solow, "Technical Change and the Aggregate Production Function," *Review of Economics and Statistics* 34 (August 1957), pp. 312-320; Kendrick,

Productivity Trends; and Edward F. Denison, *Why Growth Rates Differ*, (Washington: The Brookings Institution, 1967).

12. See again the excellent article by Zvi Griliches, "Cost Allocation in Railroad Regulation," *The Bell Journal of Economics and Management Science* 3 (Spring 1972), pp. 26-41.

13. Ibid.

14. See J.T. Kneafsey, "Costing in Railroad Operations: A Proposed Methodology," processed, MIT Report for the Federal Railroad Administration, U.S. Department of Transportation, December 1973.

15. For this reason, microeconomic theory texts which deal with the characteristics of multiproduct forms are better references than the more traditional ones. For example, see Thomas H. Naylor and John M. Vernon, *Microeconomics and Decision Models of the Firm* (New York: Harcourt, Brace & World, Inc., 1969).

16. This adaptation is treated in Theodore E. Keeler, "Railroad Costs, Return to Scale, and Excess Capacity: A Neoclassical Analysis," Working Paper No. 35, Department of Economic, University of California, Berkeley, April 1973.

17. Ibid.

18. A good reference on this topic is James M. Henderson and Richard E. Quandt, *Microeconomic Theory* (New York: McGraw Hill, 1958), which has been one of the more definitive works in microeconomics during the last decade. Also, a text which the author has used in teaching is Thomas H. Naylor and John M. Vernon, *Microeconomics and Decision Models of the Firm* (New York: Harcourt, Brace & World, Inc., 1969).

19. This analysis is based on one developed by J. Meyer, M. Peck, J. Stenason, and C. Zwick in *The Economics of Competition in the Transportation Industries* (Cambridge: Harvard University Press, 1959).

20. Numerous citations dealing with wastes and inefficiencies among the independent regulatory commissions could be mentioned. Three important books of this group include: Paul W. MacAvoy, ed., *The Crisis of the Regulatory Commissions* (New York: W.W. Norton & Co., Inc., 1970); William M. Capron, *Technological Change in Regulated Industries* (Washington: The Brookings Institution, 1971); and Ann F. Friedlaender, *The Dilemma of Freight Transport Regulation* (Washington: The Brookings Institution, 1969).

5 National Transportation Policy and the Transportation Firm

Even though national transportation policy is an extremely important matter, it is difficult to identify its exact nature. Congress initially promulgates national transportation policy through its action in appropriating funds, in establishing and authorizing regulatory commissions and administrative boards, and in announcing policy guidelines. The executive branch influences national transportation policy principally through its power of appointment and through the Department of Transportation.

There are at least two types of policy, as discussed in the previous chapter: statutory policy and ad hoc or informal policy. The Transportation Act of 1920, an example of statutory policy, subjected the railroads to the complex regulation in the public utility mold that had been adopted by many states to combat the practices of local utilities. Regulation existed at that time allegedly for the purpose of controlling monopoly and restricting competition among the railroad companies.

Between 1920 and 1935, technological advances changed the transportation structure drastically. No longer was transportation a monopoly of the railroads. During the era of the Great Depression, the basis for national transportation policy became the restriction of and protection against competition. This philosophy was embodied in the Motor Carrier Act of 1935, the Civil Aeronautics Act of 1938, and the Transportation Act of 1940 as applied to water common carriers. The numerous exemptions and exceptions to these pieces of legislation reflected the obvious discomfort experienced by each of the industries covered by their respective statutory policies. The litigation arising from interpretations of these statutes has continued at an increasing pace to the present time. Needless to say, the economic costs associated with the litigation have been substantial.

The role of the common carrier in transportation is not nearly so great as in earlier decades. With the advent of various forms of noncommon carriage and other innovative endeavors, there are at least three main national policy issues which relate to the current activities of the common carrier. As suggested by Pegrum, these issues include:

1. The degree of protection which should be afforded common carriers against each other, regardless of mode. . . .
2. The protection to be afforded common carriers from those that cannot be forced into this category. . . .

3. The question of whether common carriers should be confined to common carrier transport.[1]

The ultimate resolutions of these issues will depend on the effectiveness of the institutional arrangements among the carriers, the commissions, the Department of Transportation, and in some instances, the Department of Justice. As an example of formal statutory policy, consider the following criteria originally stated in the Interstate Commerce Act of 1887, Sec. 5(2)C and amended by The Transportation Act of 1940, Sec. 5(2):

1. The effect of the proposed transaction upon adequate transportation service to the public.
2. The effect upon the public interest of the inclusion, or failure to include, other railroads in the territory involved in the proposed transaction.
3. The total fixed charges resulting from the proposed transactions.
4. The interest of the carrier employees affected.

Despite the appealing goals which appear in the statutory proclamations and despite the belated recognition of transportation as a systems problem, the impacts of the statutes are unfortunately deficient. The most significant disappointment has been the inability to implement the stated goals into practice. One author has even condensed this deficiency into three words: "Incomplete, inconsistent and indefinable."[2]

The impacts of national transportation policy are not totally negative. The narrative of the statutes does point in the right direction; awareness is perhaps a necessary first step in a tedious process, the benefits of which may still remain before us. Perhaps more important and more affirmative is that the statutory policy has established a set of standards: "it does set up goals and ideas no matter how unattainable they may be."[3]

The market structure and economic performance of firms do depend on the smoothness with which the government agencies function. If the perceived directives of different agencies overlap, as they frequently do, the firm will continue to waste expenditures on unnecessary litigation procedures. This comment pertains especially to the modal agencies in DOT vis-à-vis the independent commissions. It is extremely frustrating to witness petty (and occasionally not so petty) jurisdictional disputes between government agencies over a particular litigation case, a policy statement, or even a minor research program.

Railroad abandonment proceedings before the ICC have been cumbersome processes, although there is some evidence that efforts to expedite the proceedings began in late 1973. Even with more rapid line abandonments, there is no consensus on the savings which would accrue to the railroads. Still, it is an evident case of regulatory constraint impeding the implementation of private carrier managerial decisions. The decisions, by the way, appear to be fairly predictable. Since abandonment of rail lines is an investment (disinvestment) decision, it should be expected that the number of route miles in any year would be related to the rate of return earned in the previous year. In fact, the correlation coefficient between these two variables is -0.71 for a twenty-year sample, as Table 5-1 shows.

Previous studies on the rationalization of the U.S. railroad systems have identified two specific types of structural change: railroad line abandonments for industrial companies and railroad mergers between two companies. These two types of rationalization typically are concerned with the effects of structural change on the industry, on competing modes, on railroad employees,

Table 5-1

Miles of Railroad Line for which Application to Abandon Was Requested versus Rate of Return on Net Investment Earned during Preceding Year

Year	Route Miles Applied for Abandonment[a]	Rate of Return on Net Investment during Preceding Year[b]
1952	1,294	3.76
1953	976	4.16
1954	498	4.19
1955	976	3.28
1956	731	4.22
1957	1,190	3.95
1958	2,062	3.36
1959	1,203	2.76
1960	1,682	2.72
1961	1,140	2.13
1962	1,869	1.97
1963	1,937	2.74
1964	1,528	3.12
1965	2,224	3.16
1966	1,920	3.69
1967	860	3.90
1968	2,036	2.46
1969	2,287	2.44
1970	1,762	2.36
1971	2,450	1.73
1972	2,623	2.49
1973	–	2.95

Sources:

[a]*Annual Reports* of the Interstate Commerce Commission.

[b]*Railroad Facts*, 1963 ed. (1950-1959); *Yearbook of Railroad Facts*, 1973 ed. (1960-1973).

on the users of rail service, and finally on municipalities and states. The general purpose of the previous studies of these effects has been to evaluate the degrees of success achieved in improving the railroad network configuration. Unfortunately, the studies neither have been able to generate viable solutions nor to distinguish between the practical and inappropriate propositions put forth in the ICC testimony for individual cases. While the reasons for this lack of success are numerous, complex, and beyond the scope of this discussion, their importance should become more salient during the next few years under the implementation of the Regional Rail Reorganization Act of 1973.

An important consideration is that transportation firms normally know less about their demand characteristics than about their costs. Except for the infrequent cases where experimentation is possible, information about price, income, and cross-elasticities of demand is remarkably difficult to forecast for the future, and this statistical area is one where the staffs of the regulatory commissions can provide important research initiative.

At the present time, the consuming public spends $250 billion dollars on domestic transportation in an economy with a GNP of $1.25 trillion. Of this figure, nearly $105 billion is spent on freight transportation with railroads' share in the vicinity of $15 billion.[4] These figures do not include the value of goods-in-transit or commodities available for resale by wholesale or retail trade interests. Neither do the figures reflect the cost of ordering, storage, spoilage, and obsolescence of commodities nor the costs associated with stockouts and the distributional inefficiencies resulting from them.

In most industries, the functional area of distribution and its inherent dependence on efficiency in the railroad and motor trucking sectors play important roles in the spatial strategy of the firms and in the efficiency of their operations. The lack of interest in maintaining efficient levels of performance in the provision of transportation services by rail and by trucking may be costing the country billions of dollars annually.[5] Even putting efficiency issues aside, most carriers and shippers have very little information, or ways to procure it, on how to estimate performance standards of their operations.[6]

As a consequence of this long neglect, there appear to be real possibilities for improving the efficiency of American industry through improvements to distribution. The savings, however, will come only after we have increased our knowledge of the existing situation, the possibilities for change and, perhaps more importantly, our understanding of the institutions and the ways in which they can be changed. A major reason for the lack of progress in this area is that much of the potential for change lies outside the sphere of control of any one firm. An individual railroad, for example, has difficulty in gathering the information required, understanding the problem at its broadest level, and in exercising the control necessary to make an important change. As a result, institutional mechanisms have developed for handling most situations. Channels of communication have been established and (although they are ponderous, slow, and sometimes inefficient) they somehow perform most of the required functions. If change is to be accomplished, though, it must come from external stimuli. The federal government, in its role as regulator, mediator, and promoter for the common good, must be prepared to step in. Before this can be done, however, the full consequence of proposed actions should be understood thoroughly and be formulated in terms of the range of controls available to various government agencies.

As an example of a questionable regulatory agency action, consider a typical CAB-approved fare increase for the airline industry. During a time of energy conservation in late 1973, the airlines reduced their capacity in some long-haul city-pair markets by as much as 25 percent. The number of air passengers demanding service did not fall off, however, and the result was a fairly sharp increase in load factors (and presumably in profitability). Against this background, the CAB approved a 5 percent increase in domestic air fares effective December 1, 1973.

Another questionable practice in the airline industry pertains to the so-called mutual aid pact among the carriers. Most of the domestic scheduled airline companies signed an accord drafted in 1958 under which they agree to reimburse up to 50 percent of an affected airline's operating costs during a strike.[a] Labor union representatives claim that this agreement reduces the economics effects normally associated with a strike and thereby cushions the position of the airline company, usually resulting in the prolonging of a strike. There appears to be other sentiment that this accord provides the airline company with an unfair bargaining advantage. The Civil Aeronautics Board, perhaps with pressure from the Antitrust Division of the Department of Justice, may amend this mutual aid accord.

Antitrust cases represent an arena in which the basic structural and performance relationships are tested and analyzed in the unregulated sector of the economy. The Federal Trade Commission and the Antitrust Division of the Justice Department have been charged by the Congress with the enforcement of past statutes and the development of appropriate, new statutes which seek generally to forestall the evolvement of noncompetitive industry structures and to restrain certain types of anticompetitive behavior by firms throughout the major portion of the economy. The extent to which these agencies interact with transportation firms is ordinarily minor. Yet the overall dynamics of technological and managerial change, inflation, politics, environmental concerns, domestic and international competition, and the simple desire to do better intensify the importance of constructive coordination among the transportation agencies and the firms for which they have varying responsibilities.

---

[a]Over the fifteen-year period of the accord, Northwest Orient has been the principal beneficiary of the strike provisions. As an example of the magnitude of the strike contributions, in a strike by the Transport Workers Union against Trans World Airlines in November 1973, the airline was eligible for payments of $9.8 million each week of the strike from the other airlines as a result of the mutual aid pact.

In any discussion of antitrust policy or economic performance, the relationship of market share to monopoly power is an issue of central importance. While the calculation of market shares depends on the specification(s) of markets (no easy matter itself), the bases on which a particular share "tends to create a monopoly" is not unambiguous. In view of the meager economic theory relevant to this question and the use of rules of thumb to decide whether a particular market share would "substantially lessen competition," it may be worthwhile to examine existing methods of analysis to widen the understanding of the problem and provide better criteria for antitrust and regulatory policies. In these ways, the independent regulatory commissions face problems similar to those of the Antitrust Division of the U.S. Department of Justice.

Notes

1. Dudley F. Pegrum, "Restructuring the Transport System," in Ernest W. Williams, Jr., ed., *The Future of American Transportation* (Englewood Cliffs, N.J.: Prentice-Hall, Inc., 1971), pp. 66-67.

2. Martin T. Farris, "National Transportation Policy: Fact or Fiction?" *Quarterly Review of Economics and Business* 10 (Summer 1970), pp. 7-14.

3. Ibid., p. 13.

4. The estimates are those of the author. Comparable figures for 1972 are: GNP—$1.13 trillion; domestic transportation—$225 billion; freight transport—$100 billion; and rail transport—$14.3 billion. Sources: *Survey of Current Business*, August 1973, plus author's estimates and Transportation Association of America, *Transportation Facts and Trends*, 1972; also compare these data with Figure 1-1.

5. Ann F. Friedlaender, *The Dilemma of Freight Transport Regulation* (Washington: The Brookings Institution, 1969).

6. See U.S. DOT, Northeast Corridor Transportation Project, *Studies on the Demand for Freight Transportation*, vol. III, May 1969.

6

Transportation and the Theory of the Firm

In his 1966 presidential address to the American Economic Association, Fritz Machlup attempted to synthesize the theory of the firm but wound up extolling his own bias toward the marginalist approach of explaining firm behavior.[1] To the extent that the classical model of the theory of the firm (and the inherent assumption of profit maximization) depicts the basic instincts of business firms, Machlup is correct. But to describe the short-run behavior of increasingly complex firms in the 1970s requires an examination of alternative objectives within the theory of the firm through a relaxation of the profit maximization assumption. To present a complete catalogue of the issues involved would be too ambitious a task for this occasion, but a partial listing might be helpful. Additional empirical content also can be given to the theory of the firm by specifying certain aspects of the firm's behavior directly.

The two major revisionist approaches which have influenced the literature so far are the behavioral and the managerial.[2] The behavioral approach has focused on empirical analyses of decision processes of individual firms and incorporated the results into models of the firm. The managerial approach modifies the objective function of the firm to accommodate the results of empirical observations of individual firm behavior. Although both approaches use behavioral information, the behavioral models include explicit decision rules (often nonmaximizing) whereas the managerial approach generally contains an optimization of a specific objective function.

No longer should an objective view of the economic task be sufficient to determine behavior. Some empirical evidence should be generated to describe the way that management perceives its task and whether it has special objectives to pursue along with this task. This evidence would be especially useful in the transportation industries where peculiar and frequent changes in daily operations necessitate managerial behavior that should be more resilient and attuned to different perspectives than is the case with firms in the purely private sector. It is not necessary to build a detailed model that explains every action of the firm; rather the importance lies in discovering at least one important factor and adding it to an already existing framework.

At this point, one must examine the crucial question to which the theory of the firm should address itself and on which there is still a lack of agreement. The fundamental issue is whether the theory should explain actual decision-making in the firm. The prevailing position, and the basis for neoclassical theory, is that the actual decision process is irrelevant and that the crucial test involves any sufficient process which can yield predictions in the aggregate. The problem with this dogmatic rationale is that aggregate level explanations are becoming inadequate to handle real-world complexities. As a result, the growing uneasiness with the neoclassical approach suggests some important changes.[3]

The issues of market structure and economic performance originated primarily with applied discipline of industrial organization during the 1930s. Earlier studies of the organization of industry, of industrial behavior, and of public policy toward business had been largely institutional and narrative in approach. The development of the theories of monopolistic and imperfect competition during that period generated new attempts to analyze economic activities that did not conform very well to the then-existing models of markets and to organize a larger body of factual knowledge about industrial markets.[4]

Following the Chamberlin and Robinson contributions of the 1930s have been several significant criticisms of conventional value theory. Each criticism has transcended the imperfect competition contribution by including factors other than profit maximization in the explanations provided for firm behavior and market performance. Among these criticisms there have been Fellner's idea of limited joint profit maximization,[5] Bain's concept of entry price mechanisms,[6] the Carnegie Institute of Technology contributions on the importance of organizational and particularly "satisfactory" factors in the attainment of economic objectives (research usually associated with the names of Cyert, March, and Simon),[7] Baumol's theory of constrained sales maximization,[8] Phillip's theory of interfirm organization,[9] and Williamson's theory of managerial discretion.[10] Still more recently, various authors of game-theoretic and market-share models have provided alternatives to the classical profit maximization theory.[11]

Regulatory Theory and the Transportation Firm

In the area of regulatory theory, there have been several recent developments, largely occasioned by the impetus of *The Bell Journal of Economics and Management Science.*[12] While the emergence of these new developments stemmed primarily from the path-breaking article by Averch and Johnson in 1962,[13] regulatory theory has had only minor bearing on the operations of transportation firms. The ironic part is that hundreds of thousands of dollars are expended annually on rate hearings related to fair rates of return for transportation firms, yet in practice the rate-of-return constraint is inoperative and generally inapplicable to transportation firms, unlike the situations in both the electric power and telephone industries.

The arguments for the general case against traditional regulatory practices have been thoroughly articulated. The result has been labeled a "crisis for regulation in the United States" by Paul MacAvoy in his edited book of readings.[14] Part of the explanation for this crisis in the transportation industries is that the theory of monopoly which underlies present transport regulation is inconsistent with the empirical evidence.[15] The indications are that many services supplied by the transportation firms are not subject to regulation and very little prospect appears that such control can encompass them. Nonetheless, the areas of regulation which are appropriate to transportation firms represent a topic of important interest. The basic issues revolve around how regulatory policy has fallen short of achieving tolerably acceptable results, or to what extent it is responsible for the "crisis" in transportation, and what necessary and acceptable changes must be designed to help resolve the current dilemmas.

The theory of industrial organization establishes a number of relationships whereby market structure, if it is defined to encompass both technology and the regulatory environment, does affect market performance. While there are alternative explanations to the interactions among structure, conduct, and performance, the traditional framework for industrial organization analysis (essentially unregulated firms) suggests a flow of causation as shown in Figure 6-1.

The market structures of most regulated industries, however, involve uncommon characteristics that suggest special attention. In most cases, the minimum optimal firm size to realize economies of scale is generally so large as to preclude the existence of many small-size firms. With a given market demand, one or a few large-size firms can usually supply a market at lower unit costs than many small firms. The problem for the economy is to somehow take advantage of the economies of scale provided by large firms without incurring the misfortunes of monopoly conduct. Aside from public enterprise, this resolution can take two forms. In the first case, since the pareto-optimal pricing rule requires that price equals marginal cost, the government can regulate price and provide a lump-sum subsidy for the firm's operational losses. In a second-best world, the subsidy would be financed by taxes that introduce other allocative and distributional inefficiencies, although such transfers may lack political feasibility. The second form is a departure from the pareto-optimal rule: by imposing a rule of either price discrimination, average cost pricing, or some combination thereof, regulatory commissions set prices at a level such that the firm can earn a fair rate of return on investment. If the actual rate is considered excessive by the commission, prices can be adjusted downward. Similarly, if the rate of return is too low, an upward price adjustment may be allowed. While this fair rate of return criterion is a type of regulation that has evolved in the utility industries, its rationale is nominally used in rate hearings before the ICC and the CAB. Society apparently benefits from lower than otherwise unit costs of production without monopoly prices and the firm realizes a rate of return on its investment sufficient to attract new capital. Unfortunately, industry observations would label this as such a superficial notion since the effects of regulation will vary with different postulates of firm behavior. In the Averch-Johnson article, a

Basic Conditions	
Supply	Demand
Price elasticity and cross-elasticity Raw materials Technology Product durability Value/weight Business attitudes Unionization Location	Price elasticity Rate of growth Substitutes and cross-elasticity Marketing type Purchase method Cyclical and seasonal character Location

Market Structure	
Industry maturity Governmental participation Product differentiation Number and size distribution of sellers and buyers	Barriers to entry Cost structures Vertical integration Diversification Scale economics

Market Conduct	
Collusion Pricing strategy Product strategy Responsiveness to change	Research and innovation Advertising Legal tactics

Market Performance	
Output Growth in output Technological advance Employment	Allocative efficiency X-efficiency Equity

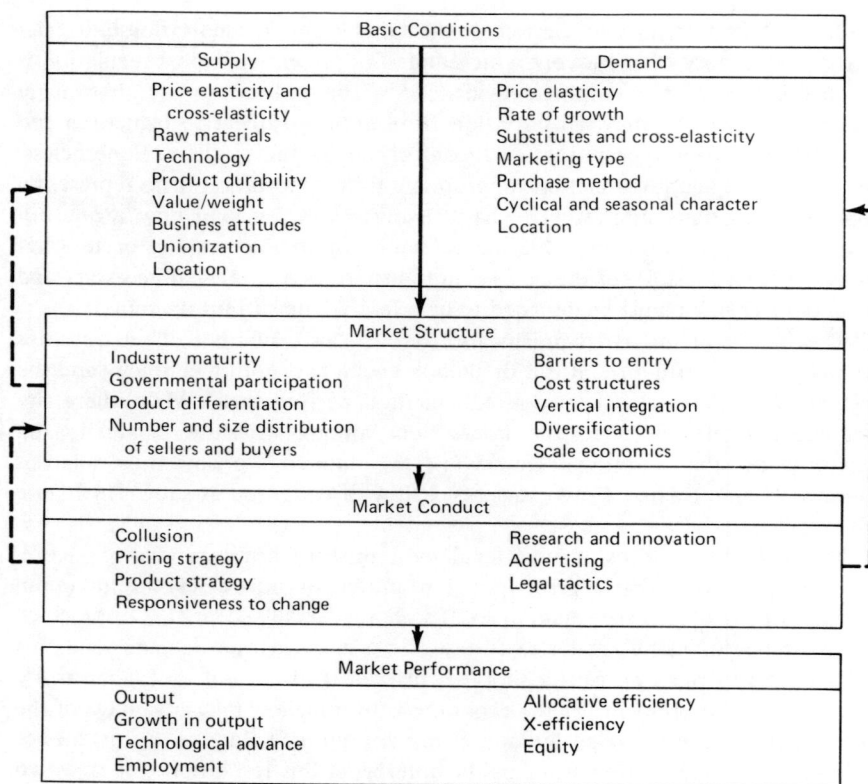

Figure 6-1. The Traditional Framework for Industrial Organization Analysis. Source: James V. Koch, *Industrial Organization and Prices* (Englewood Cliffs, N.J.: Prentice-Hall, Inc., 1974), p. 6 Reprinted by permission.

regulated profit-maximizing model was used to display a definite regulatory bias of overcapitalization.[16] In general, the overcapitalization phenomenon implied by the Averch-Johnson model and by its recent modifications describes a variety of situations that may or may not be an implication of the profit-maximizing model.[17] The major source of confusion is "inflating" or "padding" the rate base by either including in the rate-base entries which are dubious investments or the acquisition of unproductive capital.[18] As an example in the transportation industries, airline firms can easily disguise some of their advertising, administrative, and general promotion expenditures in this way.

The shortcomings of the revenue maximizing model, and the possible discretionary activity of managers suggest that any alternative theory of the firm be general enough to encompass a wide variety of cases without losing specific relevance. The revenue-maximization model and the rate of return to equity maximization model are two attempts to invoke empirical content into the theory of the firm. Both models start with certain empirical observations of the market conduct of a firm and then postulate a behavior for the firm managers through the optimization of an objective function which provides a theoretical structure to explain the empirical observations. Managerial models tend to be designed to explain the firm's behavior in certain situations and consequently lack generality. Since the effects of regulation vary with different assumptions defining the environment and alternative motivations for the firm, an assessment of regulation is much more complicated than if effects were invariant. A proper assessment could be greatly facilitated, and the responsibilities of regulatory commissions could be thoroughly defined, if a better theoretical model of the firm provided unambiguous and generalized results to the performance of transportation firms.

Two major advances in the theory of the firm have been contributed by Oliver Williamson and by Robin Marris.[19] The strength of their methodology is based on a utility analysis of the firm which yields more meaningful tradeoffs and results than heretofore traditional analysis. Marris' work is enriched by its motivational analysis and description of corporate development. However, it concentrates upon a model of growth-rate maximization that is constrained by a minimum security level, and relatively little attention is given to the more potent managerial utility model in which rate of growth is traded off for security.

Williamson's work develops a utility model of the firm that structures the effect of internal organization upon managerial goals and internal efficiency of the firm. The theory of the firm developed by Williamson is specifically designed to explain the behavior of large corporations and could be adopted to transportation firms with the appropriate modifications. An assessment of the effects of regulation and of the role of regulatory commissions is enhanced by investigating the internal structure of the corporation. As suggested in Chapter 4, the effectiveness of regulation is dependent upon the internal control of the corporation.[20]

The firm as it administers its production activity encounters a variety of market phenomena such as incomplete information, transaction costs, and uncertainty of the future. In its response to these phenomena, the managers of the firm incorporate other activities into the firm that are designed to reduce the costs associated with market failures. If market structure conditions are such that the product market of the firm is not competitive, the firm can quite easily evolve into a multifunctional enterprise. With a favorable market structure, the firm grows in size and continues to incorporate more activities into its organization. The firm may proceed to internalize externalities, integrate vertically and reduce transaction costs whenever it is profitable. In a multifunctional corporation, the traditional role of the entrepreneur is gradually transformed into that of a peak coordinator who directs the various functions of the corporation. The peak coordinator is generally considered to be motivated by profit maximization. However, interesting results of discretionary motives are revealed as the firm expands its size.

The organizational structure of the corporation is similar to the hierarchical structure of most complex organizations. The very design of a hierarchical organization tends to isolate shocks to the organization and to reduce the amount of information processing required from individuals in the organization. Williamson describes the unitary form organization as a hierarchical organization where the peak coordinator delegates all authority and decision-making.[21] As the corporation expands, it is possible that another organization with a structure similar to the original one will emerge and is integrated with the original structure by an overall peak coordinator. This method of expansion is termed *multidivisionalization*. Alternatively, the corporation could expand in a fashion that preserves the original organization form: the unitary form. This process is called *amplification* and is accomplished by introducing additional hierarchical levels.[22] Regardless of organizational form, there are inherent limits to the size of the corporation.

Williamson investigates the interaction of control loss and corporate size in the context of unitary form organization by postulating a model of the corporation which maximizes net revenue and yields expressions that determine the optimal number of hierarchical levels and the optimal size of the corporation.[23] If this model can be applied to railroad firms, it would be a valuable source of information for the ICC.

Suppose that a railroad can choose to pursue any number of managerial objectives, such as: net revenues, sales, utility (welfare), or market share, subject to any constraints imposed either by the ICC or by itself. Assume, for example, it chose to optimize its own welfare (u) subject to the ICC's requirement that taxes and a minimum profit be earned ($\Pi_R \geqslant \Pi_0 + T$). Then, the problem becomes

$$\text{Max. } u = F(s, M, F, Q) \tag{6.1}$$

subject to

$$(\Pi - M) \geqslant \Pi_0 + T \tag{6.2}$$

where:

s = span of control

α = fraction of work done by a subordinate ($0 < \alpha < 1$); an internal efficiency parameter or *compliance* factor

N_i = number of employees at the ith hierarchical level = s^{i-1}

n = number of hierarchical levels (decision variable)

p = price of output (avg. rates)

w_o = base wage rate of workers

w_i = wage rate of employees at the ith hierarchical level = $w_o \beta^{n-1} (\beta > 1)$

r = nonwage variable cost per unit output

Q = output (ton-miles) = $\theta (\alpha s)^{n-1}$

R = revenue = PQ

C = total variable cost = $\sum\limits_{i=1}^{n} wN_i + rQ$

F = staff expense

M = emoluments

Π = actual profits = $R - C - F$

Π_R = reported profits = $\Pi - M$

Π_o = minimum (after tax) profits demanded

T = taxes (where $\bar{t}$ = tax rate)

discretionary profits = $\Pi_R - \Pi_o - T$

Since $\Pi = R - C - F$, the left-hand side of the constraint becomes

$$R - C - F - M = PQ - \sum_{i=1}^{n} w_i N_i - rQ - F - M \qquad (6.3)$$

$$= P(\alpha s)^{n-1} - \sum_{i=1}^{n} w_o \beta^{n-1} s^{i-1} - r(\alpha s)^{n-1} - F - M.$$

Taking first- and second-order conditions, one can find an optimal n^* (number of hierarchical levels) as a function of: α, s, F, and M. Associated with this n^* is an optimum performance characteristic of the organization structure of the company. If this structure were to change (for instance, by a merger), then the ICC could estimate its organizational and structural impacts.

The transportation firm that is motivated by managerial discretion anticipates the behavior of the regulatory agency. For instance, managers realize that regulators set prices periodically so that the firm performance approximates a fair rate of return, especially if the firm earns short-run profits above the prevailing standard. Managers react to this possibility by imposing a safe profit constraint on their operations.

If in fact regulatory agency members do inspect expenses or costs of the firm, managers can anticipate this behavior and react by imposing their own constraint on staff expenditures so that they do not exceed some maximum proportion of total output. This action would preclude any disciplining action from the agency. If the optimal size of the firm can be determined, regulatory agencies could pinpoint excessive profits, excessive costs, or excessive output. Alternatively, if the regulatory agencies could influence organizational structure so that any changes in goal formation and internal efficiency improve market conduct and performance, less surveillance and interference by the regulatory agencies would be necessary.

Alternative Objectives in the
Transporation Firm[a]

Most models of pricing strategies in the economics literature have adhered to the assumption that business firms seek to maximize profits. Newer models of the behavior of large corporations have included a variety of assumptions about business motivation and nonmaximizing behavior in the traditional static frameworks. The developers of these new models have paid increasing attention to the nature and determinants of the forces governing the size and growth of the companies of which they are composed. As a result, the newer theoretical models of the growth of the firm are rapidly becoming more rigorous, comprehensive, and widely accepted.

Since firms in the transportation industries compete in money and capital markets with numerous other firms in both the regulated and unregulated sectors of the economy, these models of firm behavior can be applied directly to each of the transportation industries. The focus is on alternative formulations of managerial goals which transportation firms may be pursuing in practice, especially the consideration of different objective functions which the companies may be following in lieu of profit maximization. Since these models reflect the behavior of any single firm in any mode, the analysis is one of partial equilibrium which assumes the activities of all other competitors as given.[b]

The section has two general purposes. It is intended mainly to provide a frame of reference from which alternative hypotheses can be stated concerning the objectives which managers and executives employed by a representative transportation firm, say in the airline industry, may be pursuing. It also incorporates as comprehensive a list as possible of alternative objective functions

[a]This section is based on a paper by the author entitled "Objectives of the Airline Firm: Theory," Proceedings of MIT/NASA Workshop on Airline Economics and Regulation, July 1972.

[b]This restriction is severe with respect to the scope of economic questions (both analytical and practical) that can be answered, because economic analysis also seeks to investigate how systems of many firms, or of all firms, behave, interact with, and constrain each other in markets, broad sectors, and the whole economy.

and demonstrates graphically that each separate objective may result in its own unique price (fare) and output (volume) combination when equilibrium occurs.

Some Simplified Specifications of Alternative Objective Functions

Using the neoclassical goal (objective) of profit maximization as a base, one can analyze the following alternative objective functions:

A. Short-run profit maximization
B. Revenue maximization
C. Sales maximization (break-even)
D. Volume maximization
E. Cost minimization
F. Constrained sales maximization
   1. Minimum value profits
   2. Ascending buffer
   3. Descending buffer
G. Other specifications
   1. Utility maximization
   2. Growth maximization
   3. Stockholder equity maximization
   4. Security maximization
   5. Market share equalization

Each case will determine the resulting price-output combination which optimizes each alternative objective function. By nature, these models are simplistic, yet the underlying importance of the basic demand-supply relationships is reflected in the sharply different results of each model. In essence, the shapes of the revenue and cost functions (or demand and supply) determines the optimal price-output combination for each alternative. To further simplify the analyses, let us assume that the industry for discussion is the airline industry.

A. Short-Run Profit Maximization

Revenues are derived from the demand function and are depicted in Figure 6-2 (top) as a concave function (to the origin), that is, $RR = P \times Z$ where P is fare and Z represents output (or volume of passengers). Assuming that fares can be changed and that the law of demand applies ($\partial Z/\partial P < 0$), R reaches a maximum at point B.

However, to generate profits, a knowledge of costs is necessary. If costs are a

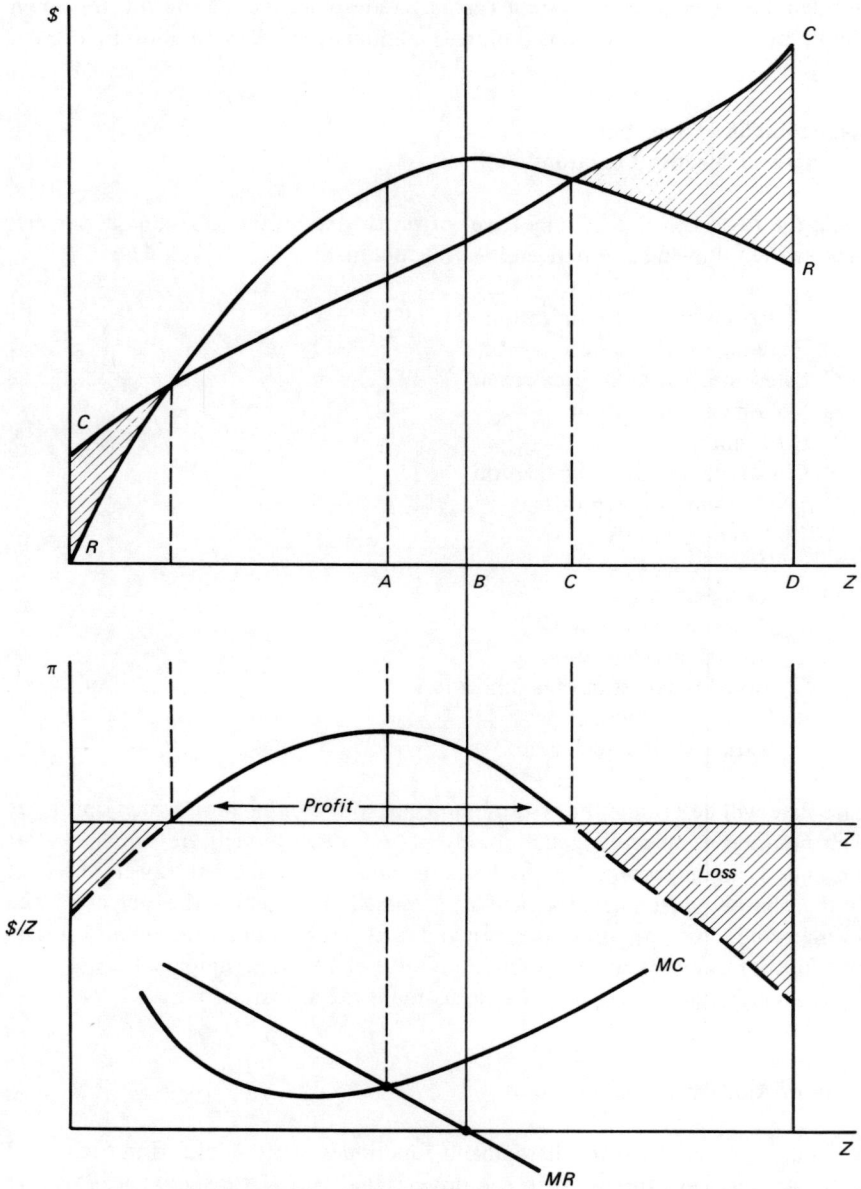

Figure 6-2. Total Dollars ($), Profits ($\pi$), and Dollars per Unit ($\$/Z$) Plotted against Output (Z)

function of volume, they can be depicted typically as *CC* in Figure 6-2 (top). Profits are simply the algebraic difference between *RR* and *CC* at each alternative level of *Z*, and are maximized when *RR* exceeds *CC* by the greatest amount (point *A* in Figure 6-2), the result being a profit curve (Figure 6-2, middle). The equating of marginal costs (*MC*) and marginal revenue (*MR*) (Figure 6-2, bottom) occurs exactly at point *A*.

B. Revenue Maximization

With the shape of the present *RR* curve, revenues are maximized at its peak (point *B* in Figure 6-2, top). This result also obtains where $MR = 0$ because additional *Z* can only occur with a decline in revenues as a result of the law of demand in operation. *MR* is simply the slope of the *RR* curve ($\partial RR/\partial z$).

C. Sales Maximization (Break-Even)

There are different variations of the sales maximization hypothesis. In this case, we are referring simply to carrying as many passengers (*Z*) out to the break-even point *C*. For reasons of market penetration, the airline may neither be interested in short-run profits nor in revenues but rather in attracting more customers.[c]

D. Volume Maximization

An extension of the sales maximization hypothesis is that an airline firm may wish to carry as many passengers as possible, even if it results in a short-term loss. The result is in effect an objective of maximizing all available capacity (point *D* in Figure 6-2, top). Note that a large loss would be incurred with the pursuit of this objective function with the present revenue and cost relationships.

E. Cost Minimization

Sometimes companies become extremely cost conscious and pursue the goal of cost minimization (point *E* in Figure 6-3). This output level occurs at the

---

[c]The typical distinction between cost in the economic sense and in the accounting sense should be made. In economic terms, *CC* includes as a component a normal rate of return to the firm in its total. However, in the strictly accounting case, *CC* is the conventional income statement figure which excludes profit.

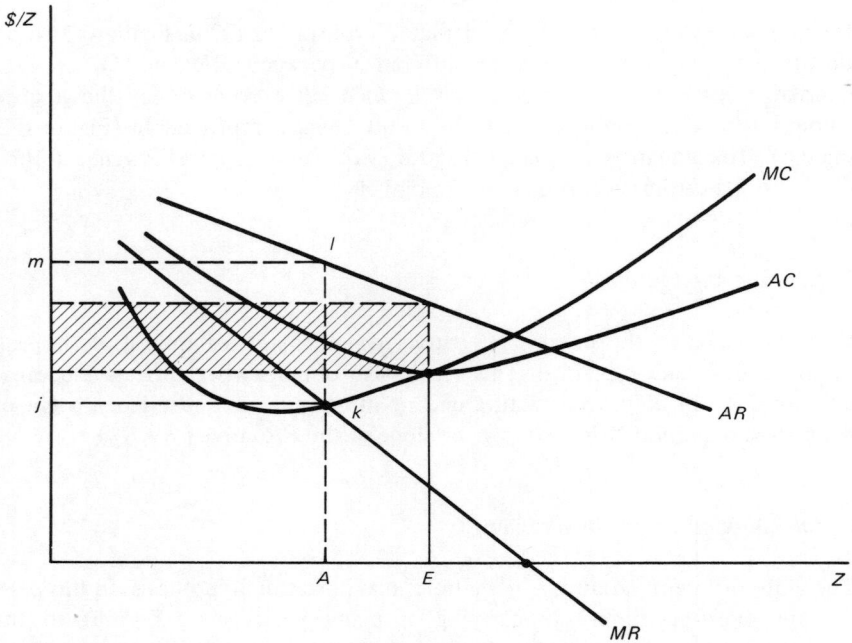

Figure 6-3. Dollars per Unit ($/Z) Plotted against Output (Z)

bottom of the average cost curve (*AC*) where *MC* = *AC*. It is an objective completely independent of demand influences, unlike the goals discussed above. A danger which companies occasionally and regrettably experience is that they may minimize themselves to death if revenue considerations are ignored. If the demand curve (*AR*) lies far below where it does in Figure 6-3, then cost minimization as a corporate objective still would not help. As it turns out in the present case, total profits are depicted by the hatched area in Figure 6-3 (as compared with *jklm*, the total profits accruing from a goal of profit maximization).

F. Constrained Sales Maximization

1. Minimum Value Profits. This hypothesis has been advanced by a number of economists with W.J. Baumol in the vanguard. In the most complete statement of this proposition, Baumol argued that firms with market power tend to maximize sales subject only to the condition that profits not fall below some specified minimum value.[24] In Figure 6-4, profits are maximized at A. However, if management feels that a certain level of profits is satisfactory or even necessary to maintain (OM in Figure 6-4, bottom) irrespective of volume (Z), then the company's goal is overfulfilled at volume OA. It can increase volume to $O(F1)$ while earning at least OM in profits, enjoying higher "sales" than it would under a short-run profit maximization policy. If the company's managers insist on earning profits of ON before seeking to satisfy other objectives such as sales maximization, they will not be in a position to increase revenues beyond the short-run profit maximizing level since the profit objective lies out of reach. The most important implication of this analysis is that if firms in the airline industry in fact strive to increase revenues for its own sake and if they require

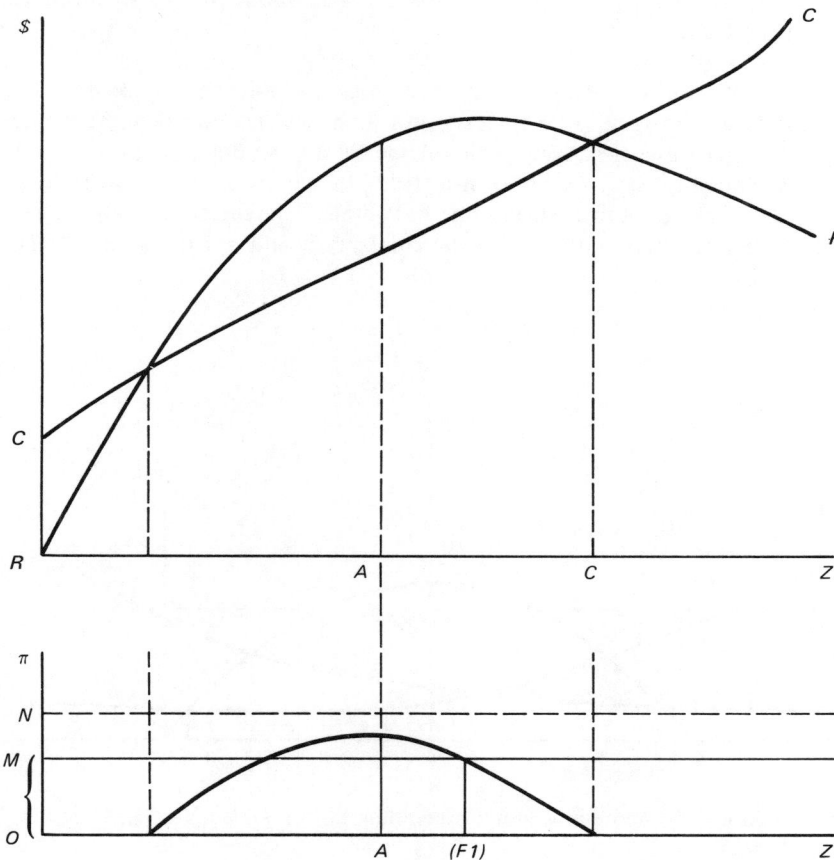

Figure 6-4. Contrained Sales Maximization

less profit to meet capital needs (for example, *OM* in Figure 6-4), then they can charge lower fares and offer more volume than they would under the goal of profit maximization. Two variations of this objective are the ascending and descending buffer objectives.

2. Ascending Buffer. In Figure 6-4, *OM* represents a "buffer" of profits which the firm desires to earn. These profits may be used for unexpected financing purposes, for dividend declarations, or for retained earnings. As long as *OM* is earned, the company will sacrifice additional profits for more sales. In Figure 6-4, *KK* represents a buffer stock of profits which increases with volume (*Z*). With more and more volume presumably they should be in a stronger position to increase dividends or to finance additional expenditures. An allowance for this growth is reflected in the rising slope of *KK* In this case the company will select volume (*F*2) in Figure 6-5, where sales are maximized subject to the buffer (*KK*) constraint.

3. Descending Buffer. Alternatively, firms may be willing to sacrifice substantial short-run profits in order to generate volume which would result in a buffer stock *LL* that varies negatively with volume. If volume during a given period is decreased sharply, say as a result of a strike, the company may wish to have a larger profit buffer at low ranges of *Z*. As volume increases, though, the tradeoff with profits becomes apparent and the company would opt for output (*F*3) in Figure 6-5.

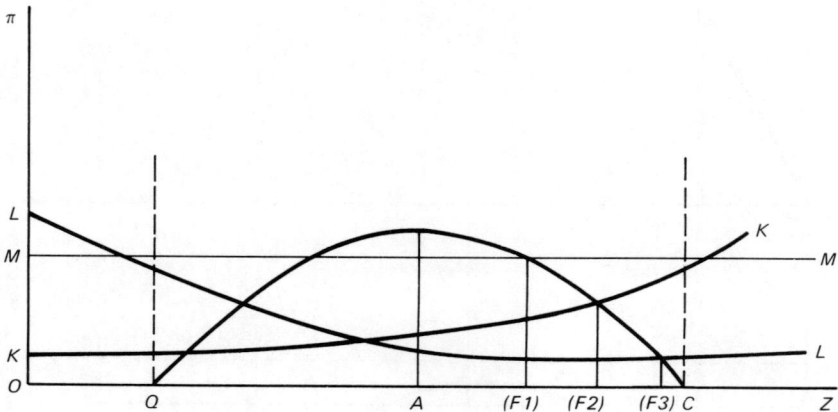

Figure 6-5. Ascending and Descending Buffer Objectives; and "Satisficing"

G. "Satisficing"

In the early 1960s, several economists in the Graduate School of Administration at the then Carnegie Institute of Technology developed the "behavioral" theory of the firm. At the heart of this theory lies the concept of "satisficing," usually attributed to the work of Herbert Simon. Essentially, satisficing refers to the fact that firms may not be maximizing at all, but rather may be pursuing a number of goals simultaneously, resulting in accepting a "satisfactory" level of profits. Graphically, this means that the firm can select any volume in Figure 6-5 as long as some satisfactory level of profits is attained. In the case of pursuing any profit at all, the range would be QC within which the firm would be "satisfied."

H. Other Specifications (Nongraphical)

Numerous other objectives could be pursued by firms in practice either individually or jointly. These goals might include the maximization of a firm's utility function, of its rate of growth in output, or of its stockholders' equity. Since ownership and management are separate functions of airlines and other large companies, an important objective to analyze might be the maximization of the management's own security and stability. Also, the companies might be satisfied with maintaining or increasing market shares as an objective independent of any other one.

The goals in this section cannot be demonstrated graphically. For those objectives which have been discussed, a summary version of each alternative volume appears in Figure 6-6.

Additional Comments on Objectives
in the Theory of the Firm

No one has yet succeeded in demonstrating conclusively whether or not airlines or other business firms behave in the ways and for the reasons postulated in the above models of selecting alternative objective functions. One obstacle to enlightenment is that the behavioral differences between long-run profit maximization and various short-run alternative goals are so subtle that econometric tests with existing data are not sufficiently powerful to discriminate among the contending hypotheses. Since it is clear that airlines do pursue one or more of these objectives in practice, the present state of knowledge certainly must be extended through more sophisticated econometric research and by more detailed case studies than any heretofore attempted.

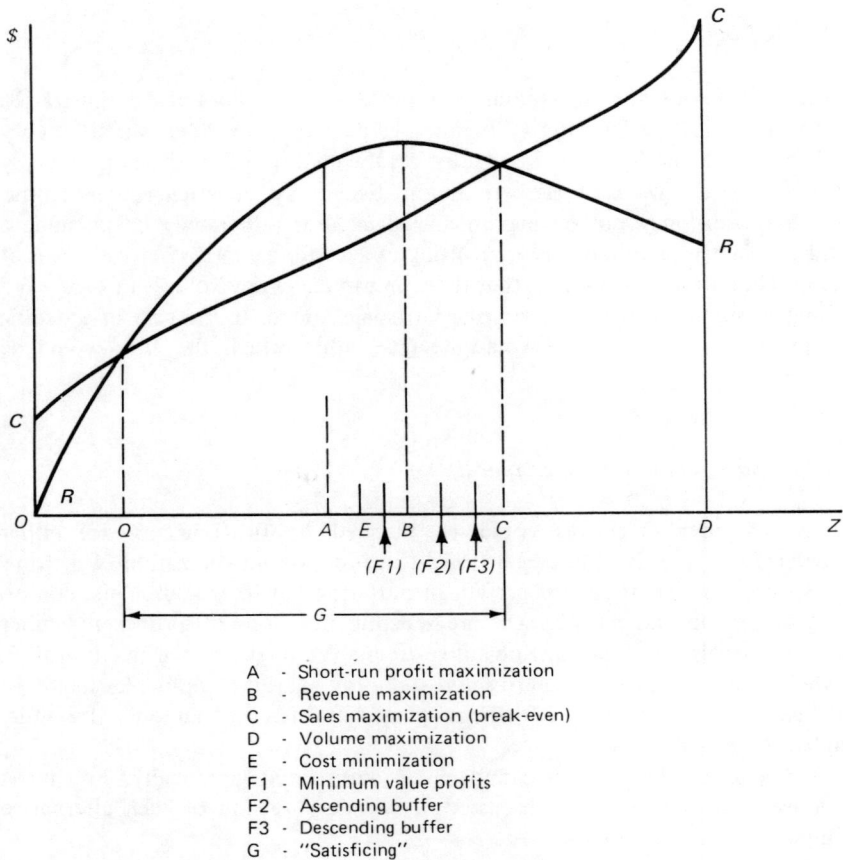

A - Short-run profit maximization
B - Revenue maximization
C - Sales maximization (break-even)
D - Volume maximization
E - Cost minimization
F1 - Minimum value profits
F2 - Ascending buffer
F3 - Descending buffer
G - "Satisficing"

Figure 6-6. Objectives of the Airline Firm—Summary

Notes

1. Fritz Machlup, "Theories of the Firm: Marginalist, Behavioral, Managerial," *American Economic Review* 57 (March 1967), pp. 1-33. This article was a sequel to the spirited debate on the usefulness of the classical model between Richard Lester and Machlup in the 1940s. See R.A. Lester, "Shortcomings of Marginal Analyses for Wage-Employment Problems," *American Economic Review* 36 (March 1946), pp. 63-82, and F. Machlup, "Marginal Analyses and Empirical Research," *American Economic Review* 36 (September 1946), pp. 519-54.

2. For an excellent summary of these approaches, see Richard M. Cyert and Charles L. Hedrick, "Theory of the Firm: Past, Present, and Future: An Interpretation," *Journal of Economic Literature*, 10 (June 1972), pp. 398-412.

3. Ibid.

4. The most significant contributions during this period were Edward Chamberlin, *The Theory of Monopolistic Competition* (Cambridge: Harvard University Press, 1933) and Joan Robinson, *The Economics of Imperfect Competition*, (London: The Macmillan Company, 1933).

5. William Fellner, *Competition among the Few* (New York: Augustus M. Kelly, 1949).

6. Joe S. Bain, *Barriers to New Competition* (Cambridge: Harvard University Press, 1956); also see his *Industrial Organization*, 2nd ed. (New York: John Wiley & Sons, Inc., 1968).

7. See: Richard M. Cyert and James G. March, "Organizational Structure and Pricing Behavior in an Oligopolistic Market," *American Economic Review* 45 (March 1955), pp. 38-55; also their *A Behavioral Theory of the Firm* (Englewood Cliffs, N.J.: Prentice-Hall, Inc., 1963); and Herbert A. Simon, *Models of Man* (New York: John Wiley and Son, 1957), esp. Chs. 14 and 15.

8. William J. Baumol, *Business Behavior, Value, and Growth*, (New York: Macmillan, 1959).

9. Almarin Phillips, *Market Structure, Organization and Performance: An Essay on Price Fixing and Combinations in Restraint of Trade* (Cambridge, Mass.: Harvard University Press, 1962).

10. Oliver E. Williamson, *The Economics of Discretionary Behavior: Managerial Objectives in a Theory of the Firm* (Chicago: Markham, 1967).

11. For a discussion of these models, see Thomas J. Naylor and John M. Vernon, *Microeconomics and Decision Models of the Firm* (New York: Harcourt, Brace and World, Inc., 1969), Chs. 11-17.

12. See W. Baumol and A. Klevorick, "Input Choices and Rate of Return Regulation: An Overview of the Discussion," *The Bell Journal of Economics and Management Science* 1 (Autumn 1970), pp. 162-190; E. Bailey and J. Malone, "Resource Allocation and the Regulated Firm," *The Bell Journal of Economics and Management Science* 1 (Spring 1970), pp. 129-42; and D.L. McNicol, "The Comparative Statics Properties of the Theory of the Regulated Firm," *The Bell Journal of Economics and Management Science* 4 (Autumn 1973), pp. 428-53.

13. Harvey Averch and Leland Johnson, "Behavior of the Firm under Regulatory Constraint," *American Economic Review* 52 (December 1962), pp. 1053-69.

14. Paul W. MacAvoy, *The Crisis of the Regulatory Commissions* (New York: W.W. Norton and Co., 1970).

15. See Dudley F. Pegrum, "Restructuring the Transport System," in Ernest W. Williams, Jr., ed., *The Future of American Transportation* (Englewood Cliffs, N.J.: Prentice-Hall, Inc., 1971), Ch. 3.

16. Averch and Johnson, "Behavior of the Firm," p. 1058.

17. Baumol and Klevorick, "Input Choices."

18. Ibid.

19. Oliver E. Williamson, *Corporate Control and Business Behavior: An Inquiry into the Effects of Organization Form on Enterprise Behavior* (Englewood Cliffs, N.J.: Prentice-Hall, Inc., 1970); and Robin Marris, *The Economic Theory of "Managerial" Capitalism* (1964; rpt. New York: Basic Books, 1968).

20. See Williamson, *Corporate Control*, p. 4.

21. Ibid., Ch. 6.

22. Ibid., Ch. 7.

23. See Ibid., Ch. 2. Also, discussions with the Charles Mueller on this point were helpful.

24. See William J. Baumol, *Business Behavior, Value and Growth* rev. ed. (New York: Harcourt, Brace and World, 1967), pp. 45-82 and 86-104.

7
Conclusion—Transportation Firms in the Long Run

The individual desire for success has been strongly rooted in the annals of American history. More recently, however, an increasing number of individuals have been questioning both the reality and the validity of our national convictions to succeed and to espouse the conventional work ethic. Our national mythology has been geared over the decades to the pursuits of hard work, social mobility, industriousness, and inadmissable exploitation. In contrast to this ethos are the messages crystallized from the resonances of our pantheon of folk heroes: losses of economic opportunity for many lower income individuals; ethnic inequities; a deterioration in the process of justice; and an erosion of the deferences given to human dignity. It is also unlikely that recent events in the public sector will alleviate any misapprehensions about access to success through federal careers. Thus the basic problem and lack of a coherent rationale for personal fulfillment through achievement have become even more magnified.

Fewer and fewer people seem to be rationally convinced that success is worth the trouble. As a result, enthusiasm appears to be lacking across the board: in industry, in public service, in entrepreneurial endeavors, even perhaps in education. The paranoias associated with goals, meaning, and the fundamental understanding of purpose have seeped into our concept of work.

Where then can individuals discover worthwhile incentives? My observations suggest that they certainly will not find, with a few exceptions, these incentives in the railroad industry; or for that matter in the motor trucking industry. Perhaps they might find some meaningful pursuits in the airline industry, but probably only because the industry is relatively "new" and still exhibits a characteristic of glamour. There is no question that the dullness and lack of showcase efforts in the pipeline and water carrier industries have relegated these industries to the background.[a] Only recently in the urban transit industry has a flurry of innovation in new systems sparked fresh incentives.

It is precisely this luster of glamour which has been lost by the railroad firms and is eroding in the airline industry. While motor trucking firms never have possessed this ingredient, the attraction of the entrepreneurial motive coupled with relatively low entry requirements has been sufficient for that industry to be profitable. Whether its participants are innovators is an unknown issue.

---

[a]The showcase passenger trains of many nationalized railroads are probably the most frequently cited examples of the benefits of nationalized systems. The promotional impacts of these trains are substantial despite the fact that they only account for a small percentage of nationalized train service and that huge subsidies are involved. As an indication of the

A basic tenet of this section is that the general demise in the transportation industries has been caused by secular factors and in turn these cause a decline in the attractiveness of the industries and hence in the qualities of the individuals who staff them. Basic questions need to be answered: Why do individuals seek employment in transportation today? What kinds of individuals are these people? What motivates them?

In the transportation industries, the concept of entrepreneur is hardly applicable nowadays. The transportation firm executive is surely not the "sedentary merchant" who was the key figure of economic progress in the early modern period. Nor is he the "undertaker" of economic activity for which the Elizabethan age is famous,[1] nor the "captain of industry" at the brink of the Industrial Revolution. Rather, he might be characterized by the ineuphonious term "business man." This term generally embraces risk-taking, policy-formulation, management, and control. It also embraces a great deal more, especially at subordinate levels of business organizations where administrative tasks acquire a more routine tenor.

As long as executives do not make costly and rash errors of judgment in forecasting the current and future activities of rival firms, one can assume that these forecasts can be made rationally. Institutional arrangements assist in this forecasting process. For example, each transportation industry has trade journals which keep firms informed as to the growth plans of rivals and provide forecasts of future outputs (and often prices). In a world of uncertainty, rational forecasts do not imply perfect foresight, but rather an orderly process of registering expectations.[2]

The corporate mind may still not be as rational as microeconomic theory assumes. Executive security, growth, and other variations of the maximization pursuits may be only illusions. This possibility has been articulated by one writer

comparative performance of domestic railroads to nationalized systems (plus the Canadian Pacific), the following statistics are presented:

System	Subsidy (Millions)	Net Income After Subsidy (Millions)	Average # Employees Per Track Mile	Ratio of Labor Costs to Revenues (Excluding Subsidies)
United States	$ 34	$ 347	2.7	52%
Canadian Pacific	22	70	2.4	52%
Canadian National	76	(24)	2.9	67%
Netherlands	32	(79)	14.2	80%
Great Britain	180	(39)	20.7	71%
French National	1,184	0	12.9	84%
German Federal	831	(764)	22.1	96%
Italian State	470	(663)	19.0	135%
Japanese National	unknown	(752)	32.9	55%

Source: Compiled from Association of American Railroads, "U.S. Railroads Vs. Nationalized Operations," December 1973, pp. 5-7.

in the following way: "When a business statesman makes public speeches, he has to talk in terms of social responsibility and long-term profit maximization, but the truth—the deep secret he can never admit to anyone except the lady who shares his pillow—is that he is a short-term profit maximizer."[3]

In principle, individuals seek productivity, prosperity, abundance, employment, and what might be called pleasure. The psychology behind this principle is represented by needs for self-gratification, recognition, and compensation. If in the transportation industries pleasure means only "putting in time" (casual and frequent observations have suggested this to be so), these needs are not fulfilled. Employees and even many executives of practically all transportation firms transfer their existence to the surrogate things outside their work days. The employees then are alienated.[4]

It is an elementary principle of large organizations that opportunities must be available to promote employees through the ranks by testing their managerial capacities and allowing for errors in their performance at levels which would not severely harm the firm itself. It is essential for survival that transportation firms develop this capability in the future. Only then can the presence of desirable participation, organization, and fulfillment among its employees and management sustain the viability of these firms and the existence of their operations as corporate entities.

Concluding Comments

Performance by firms in the domestic transportation industries has been widely criticized—largely because of poor regulation and a gradual demise in incentives within the industries. Such confessions of inadequacy should be a spur to the development of new solutions, or alternatives for, the traditional lack of economic analysis in these industries. While the internal industry problems require a lengthy, systematic, and thorough examination well beyond the scope of these comments, the eventual solution will partially be the result of adaptive responses by the transportation firms to their existing conditions and perceived alternatives. No cursory treatment of these problems is helpful, except for isolating the issues and committing resources toward the search for a solution.

On the regulatory issue, however, there are policy actions and research tasks which can be undertaken rather easily and which should represent positive social investments. In this category would fall the recommendations of research pursuits discussed earlier, especially in Chapters 3 and 4. On the basis of these discussions, some concluding and summarizing observations can be made:

1. Since firms in the transportation industries compete for loans and investment funds in the same money and capital markets as unregulated firms, the expected rates of return to investor in the transportation firms must approach

those anticipated by investors in the unregulated firms, ceterus paribus; or else transportation firms will continue to suffer in these markets.

2. Not only are transportation firms competing for financial resources with the unregulated firms, but they also compete with the unregulated firms in similar labor resource markets, for example, for management resources, for office and clerical workers, and for skilled trade union workers.

3. In the transportation industries, a basic conflict prevails between the regulatory activities of promoting competition versus the insular interests of each transportation mode.

4. The publicly stated goals of national transportation policy may be internally inconsistent and consequently inhibit innovation by transportation firms.

5. While the results of the empirical tests of some hypotheses in the industrial organization field (namely, the unregulated sector) have not been conclusive to date, statistical tests of these identical hypotheses with transportation industries' data (which should be made available) might very well be conclusive. By confirming or rejecting the hypothesis under testing, the transportation analyst or regulatory agency at least can provide some additional insight on the probable impacts of changes in market structure on industrial performance.

6. If the independent regulatory agencies desire to carry out their statutory responsibilities seriously, then their staffs should expend substantially more energies and finances on examining the linkages between market structures and economic performance in the transportation industries. Understandably, because of the limited funds which currently are allocated to the regulatory staffs, it is beyond the horizons of their expertise to examine in substantive detail all the subtleties required for the empirical verification and for the determination of the expected behavior of transportation firms. Nevertheless, any steps in this direction by the regulatory staffs should bring positive payoffs.

Market structure and economic performance are instrumental variables in evaluating the assumptions about industrial economics and in constructing rational public policies toward business firms:

Supposedly, antitrust laws, direct regulation, and other restrictions on competition are designed to improve market performance by affecting market structure and conduct. Clearly, it is essential to know how structure affects performance.[5]

This identical, essential link is no less true in the transportation industries and, it seems to this author, should be one of the basic inquiries for the agencies responsible for regulating transportation.

The obvious practical problem is how to measure the elements and dimensions of market structure and industrial performance. On such a basic concept as output, there is sharp disagreement among transportation economists as to the appropriate measure—whether it be the railroad industry, the motor trucking industry, or the airline industry. Moreover, even within an industry, the airline industry as an example, there is the difficulty of matching the units for quantity demanded and for quantity supplied.

As one might expect, the inferences which can be drawn from much empirical research are sensitive to the particular measures chosen to depict the variables under examination. Another equally perplexing problem is that of specifying the particular relationships among subsets of these variables. A final caution stems from the dangers inherent in making interindustry comparisons and slick inferences. The danger at this extreme lies in the neatness of identifications. Yet somewhere between this neatness and the current state of affairs, there hopefully is a balance.

Notes

1. See J.W. Gough, *The Rise of the Entrepreneur* (New York: Shocken Books, Inc., 1969), p. 284.

2. For applications of this concept, see R.E. Lucas, Jr., and E.C. Prescott, "Investment under Uncertainty," *Econometrics* 39 (September 1971), pp. 659-81; and E.C. Prescott, "Market Structure and Monopoly Profits: A Dynamic Theory," *Journal of Economic Theory* 6 (December 1973), pp. 546-57.

3. Leonard Silk, "Multinational Morals," *New York Times*, March 5, 1974, p. 33. © 1974 by The New York Times Company. Reprinted by permission. Of course, when the "statesman" is female, Mr. Silk might have to modify his statement.

4. For a discussion on the more aggregative implications of alienation, see Edwin G. Dolan, "Alienation, Freedom and Economic Organization," *Journal of Political Economy* 79 (September/October 1971), pp. 1084-94.

5. John M. Vernon, *Market Structure and Industrial Performance: A Review of Statistical Findings* (Boston: Allyn and Bacon, Inc., 1972), p. 30.

Selected Bibliography

Selected Bibliography

Adelman, M.A. "The Measurement of Industrial Concentration," in Heflebower, R.B. and G.W. Stocking, eds., *Readings in Industrial Organization and Public Policy* (Homewood, Ill.: Richard D. Irwin, Inc., 1958).

Altman, Edward I. "Predicting Railroad Bankruptcies in America," *The Bell Journal of Economics and Management Science* 4 (Spring 1973), pp. 184-211.

Averch, H. and L.L. Johnson. "Behavior of the Firm Under Regulatory Constraint," *American Economic Review* 52 (December 1962), pp. 1052-69.

Bain, Joe S. *Industrial Organization*, 2nd ed. (New York: John Wiley & Sons, Inc., 1968).

_____. *Essays on Price Theory and Industrial Organization* (Boston: Little, Brown, and Company, 1972).

Bain, Donald. *The Case against Private Aviation* (New York: Cowles, 1969).

Baumol, W.J. *Business Behavior, Value, and Growth* (New York: Macmillan, 1959).

_____. "The Theory of Expansion of the Firm," *American Economic Review* 52 (December 1962), pp. 1078-87.

Boyle, Stanley E. *Industrial Organization: An Empirical Approach* (New York: Holt, Rinehart and Winston, Inc., 1972).

Capron, William M., ed. *Technological Change in Regulated Industries* (Washington: The Brookings Institution, 1971).

Caves, Richard E. *Air Transport and Its Regulators: An Industry Study* (Cambridge, Mass.: Harvard University Press, 1962).

Cyert, Richard M. and James G. March. *A Behavioral Theory of the Firm* (Englewood Cliffs, N.J.: Prentice-Hall, Inc., 1963).

Daughen, Joseph R. and Peter Binzen. *The Wreck of the Penn Central* (Boston: Little, Brown, and Company, 1971).

Deakin, B.M. and T. Seward. *Productivity in Transport: A Study of Employment, Capital, Output, Productivity and Technical Change* (London: Cambridge University Press, 1969).

Eads, George C. *The Local Service Airline Experiment* (Washington: The Brookings Institution, 1972).

Engwall, Lars. *Models of Industrial Structure* (Lexington, Mass.: Lexington, Books, D.C. Heath and Co., 1973).

Fogel, Robert William. *Railroads and American Economic Growth: Essays in Econometric History* (Baltimore, Md.: The Johns Hopkins Press, 1964).

Friedlaender, Ann F. *The Dilemma of Freight Transport Regulation* (Washington: The Brookings Institution, 1969).

Fromm, Gary, ed. *Transport Investment and Economic Development* (Washington: The Brookings Institution, 1965).

Fruhan, William E. Jr. *The Fight for Competitive Advantage: A Study of the United States Domestic Trunk Air Carriers* (Cambridge, Mass.: Harvard University Press, 1972).

Gold, Bela. *Explorations in Managerial Economics: Productivity, Costs, Technology and Growth* (New York: Basic Books, 1971).

Grabowski, Harry and Dennis Mueller. "Industrial Organization: The Role and Contribution of Econometrics," *American Economic Review* 60 (May 1970), pp. 100-108.

Griliches, Zvi. "Cost Allocation in Railroad Regulation," *The Bell Journal of Economics and Management Science* 3 (Spring 1972), pp. 26-41.

Hilton, George W. "The Basic Behavior of Regulatory Commissions," *Papers and Proceedings of the American Economic Association* 62 (May 1972), pp. 47-54.

Hirschman, Albert O. *Exit, Voice and Loyalty: Responses to Decline in Firms, Organizations, and States* (Cambridge, Mass.: Harvard University Press, 1972).

Hunt, H.G. *Industrial Economics* (London: Pergamon Press, 1965).

Imel, Blake, Michael R. Behr and Peter G. Helmberger. *Market Structure and Performance: The U.S. Food Processing Industries*(Lexington, Mass.: Lexington Books, D.C. Heath and Co., 1972).

Jackson, Raymond. "The Consideration of Economies in Merger Cases," *Journal of Business* 43 (October 1970), pp. 439-47.

Johnson, James C. *Trucking Mergers: A Regulatory Viewpoint* (Lexington, Mass.: Lexington Books, D.C. Heath and Co., 1973).

Jordan, William A. *Airline Regulation in America: Effects and Imperfections* (Baltimore, Md.: The Johns Hopkins Press, 1970).

Kahn, Alfred E. *The Economics of Regulation: Principles and Institutions*. Vol. I. *Economic Principles* (New York: John Wiley & Sons, Inc., 1970).

Kelly, Eamon M. *The Profitability of Growth through Mergers* (University Park, Pa.: Pennsylvania State University, 1967).

Klevorick, Alvin K. "The 'Optimal' Fair Rate of Return," *The Bell Journal of Economics and Management Science* 2 (Spring 1971), pp. 122-53.

Kuenne, Robert E. *Microeconomic Theory of the Market Mechanism: A General Equilibrium Approach* (New York: Macmillan, 1968).

Leibenstein, Harvey. "Organizational or Frictional Equilibria, X-Efficiency, and the Rate of Innovation," *Quarterly Journal of Economics* 83 (November 1969), pp. 600-623.

MacAvoy, Paul W. *The Economic Effects of Regulation: The Trunk-Line Railroad Cartels and the Interstate Commerce Commission before 1900* (Cambridge, Mass.: The M.I.T. Press, 1965).

MacAvoy, Paul W., ed. *The Crisis of the Regulatory Commissions* (New York: W.W. Norton and Co., Inc., 1970).

MacAvoy, Paul W. and James Sloss. *Regulation of Transport Innovation: The ICC and Unit Coal Trains to the East Coast* (New York: Random House, 1967).

McGuire, Joseph W. *Theories of Business Behavior* (Englewood Cliffs, N.J.: Prentice-Hall, Inc., 1963).

McNicol, David L. "The Comparative Statics Properties of the Theory of the Regulated Firm," *The Bell Journal of Economics and Management Science* 4 (Autumn 1973), pp. 428-53.

Mann, H.M. "Seller Concentration, Barriers to Entry and Rates of Return in Thirty Industries, 1950-60," *Review of Economics and Statistics* 48 (August 1966), pp. 296-307.

Mansfield, Edwin. *Industrial Research and Technological Innovation* (New York: W.W. Norton and Co., Inc., 1968).

_____. *The Economics of Technological Change* (New York: W.W. Norton and Co., Inc., 1968).

_____. "Size of Firm, Market Structure, and Innovation," *Journal of Political Economy* 121 (December 1963), pp. 556-576.

_____. "Industrial Research and Development Expenditures," *Journal of Political Economy* 122 (June 1964), pp. 319-40.

Mansfield, Edwin, ed. *Microeconomics: Selected Readings* (New York: W.W. Norton and Co., Inc., 1971).

_____. *Defense, Science and Public Policy* (New York: W.W. Norton and Co., Inc., 1968).

_____. *Monopoly Power and Economic Performance: The Problem of Industrial Concentration* (New York: W.W. Norton and Co., Inc., 1964).

Marcus, M. "Advertising and Changes in Concentration," *Southern Economic Journal* 36 (October 1969), pp. 117-21.

Marris, Robin. *The Economic Theory of "Managerial" Capitalism* (1964; rpt. New York: Basic Books, 1968).

Marris, Robin and Adrian Wood, eds. *The Corporate Economy: Growth, Competition and Innovative Potential* (Cambridge, Mass.: Harvard University Press, 1971).

Mason, Edward S., ed. *The Corporation in Modern Society* (Cambridge, Mass.: Harvard University Press, 1961).

Meyer, John R., Merton J. Peck, John Stenason and Charles Zwick. *The Economics of Competition in the Transportation Industries* (Cambridge, Mass.: Harvard University Press, 1960).

Meyer, John R. and Mahlon R. Straszheim. *Techniques of Transport Planning.* Vol. I. *Pricing and Project Evaluation* (Washington: The Brookings Institution, 1971).

National Bureau of Economic Research. *Transportation Economics* (New York: Columbia University Press, 1965).

Naylor, Thomas J. and John M. Vernon. *Microeconomics and Decision Models of the Firm* (New York: Harcourt, Brace and World, Inc., 1969).

Nelson, Richard R., Merton J. Peck and Edward D. Kalachek. *Technology, Economic Growth and Public Policy* (Washington: The Brookings Institution, 1967).

Nordhaus, William D. *Invention, Growth and Welfare: A Theoretical Treatment of Technological Change* (Cambridge, Mass.: The M.I.T. Press, 1969).

Phillips, Almarin. *Market Structure, Organization and Performance: An Essay on Price Fixing and Combinations in Restraint of Trade* (Cambridge, Mass.: Harvard University Press, 1962).

_____ . *Technology and Market Structure: A Study of the Aircraft Industry* (Lexington, Mass.: Lexington Books, D.C. Heath and Co., 1971).

Phillips, Charles F. Jr. *The Economics of Regulation: Theory and Practice in the Transportation and Public Utility Industries* (1965; rpt. Homewood, Ill.: Richard D. Irwin, Inc., 1969).

Quandt, Richard E. *The Demand for Travel: Theory and Measurement* (Lexington, Mass.: Lexington Books, D.C. Heath and Co., 1970).

The Ralph Nader Study Group. *The Interstate Commerce Omission* (New York: Grossman Publishers, 1970).

Rubin, Paul H. "The Expansion of Firms," *Journal of Political Economy* 81 (July/August 1973), pp. 936-49.

Sampson, Roy J. "Inherent Advantages under Regulation," *Papers and Proceedings of the American Economic Review* 62 (May 1972), pp. 55-61.

Sampson, Roy J. and Martin T. Farris. *Domestic Transportation: Practice, Theory and Policy* (1966; rpt. Boston: Houghton Mifflin Company, 1971).

Scherer, F.M. *Industrial Market Structure and Economic Performance* (Chicago: Rand McNally and Co., 1970).

Schmookler, Jacob. *Invention and Economic Growth* (Cambridge, Mass.: Harvard University Press, 1966).

Seashore, Stanley E. *Group Cohesiveness in the Industrial Work Group* (Ann Arbor, Mich.: University of Michigan Press, 1954).

Seneca, Rosalind S. "Inherent Advantage, Costs, and Resource Allocation in the Transportation Industry," *American Economic Review* 63 (December 1973), pp. 945-56.

Shepherd, William G. *Market Power and Economic Welfare* (New York: Random House, 1970).

Sherman, Roger. *Oligopoly: An Empirical Approach* (Lexington, Mass.: Lexington Books, D.C. Heath and Co., 1972).

Silberman, I.H. "On Lognormality as a Summary Measure of Concentration," *American Economic Review* 57 (December 1967), pp. 807-830.

Simon, Herbert H. and C.P. Bonini. "The Size Distribution of Firms," *American Economic Review* 48 (September 1958), pp. 607-17.

Straszheim, Mahlon R. *The International Airline Industry* (Washington: The Brookings Institution, 1969).

Vernon, John M. *Market Structure and Industrial Performance: A Review of Statistical Findings* (Boston: Allyn and Bacon, Inc., 1972).

Walters, A.A. *Integration in Freight Transport* (London: The Institute of Economic Affairs, 1968).

Weston, J. Fred. *The Role of Mergers in the Growth of Large Firms* (Berkeley, Calif.: University of California Press, 1953).

Weston, J. Fred and Stanley I. Ornstein, eds. *The Impact of Large Firms on the U.S. Economy* (Lexington, Mass.: Lexington Books, D.C. Heath and Co., 1973).

Weston, J. Fred and Sam Peltzman, eds. *Public Policy toward Mergers* (Pacific Palisades, Calif.: Goodyear, 1969).

Williamson, Oliver E. *The Economics of Discretionary Behavior: Managerial Objectives in a Theory of the Firm* (Chicago: Markham, 1967).

_____ . *Corporate Control and Business Behavior: An Inquiry into the Effects of Organization Form on Enterprise Behavior* (Englewood Cliffs, N.J.: Prentice-Hall, Inc., 1970).

_____ . "The Vertical Integration of Production: Market Failure Considerations," *Papers and Proceedings of the American Economic Association* 61 (May 1971), pp. 112-23.

Zajac, E.E. "A Geometric Treatment of Averch-Johnson's Behavior of the Firm Model," *American Economic Review* 60 (March 1970), pp. 117-25.

Zellner, Arnold, ed. *Readings in Economic Statistics and Econometrics* (Boston: Little, Brown, and Company, 1968).

Index

Index

About the Author

James T. Kneafsey received the Ph.D. in economics from Ohio State University in 1971. He has developed and taught transportation courses in the Department of Economics at the University of Pittsburgh, and now in the Transport Systems Division of the Massachusetts Institute of Technology. Dr. Kneafsey's teaching and research interests center on transportation economics, industrial organization, and applied econometrics. His publications cover the industrial organization of the transportation industries, mergers in the railroad industry, air transport economics, and a wide range of multi-modal studies in transportation systems planning. Dr. Kneafsey has been a consultant to various regulatory commissions, corporations, and research firms engaged in the analysis of transportation.